Multimedia Learning

For hundreds of years, verbal messages – such as lectures and printed lessons – have been the primary means of explaining ideas to learners. In *Multimedia Learning*, Richard Mayer explores ways of going beyond the purely verbal by combining words and pictures for effective teaching. Multimedia encyclopedias have become the latest addition to students' reference tools, and the World Wide Web is full of messages that combine words and pictures. Do these forms of presentation help learners? If so, what is the best way to design multimedia messages for optimal learning?

Drawing on ten years of research, the author provides a cognitive theory of multimedia learning and seven principles for the design of multimedia messages. In short, this book summarizes research aimed at realizing the promise of multimedia learning – that is, the potential of using words and pictures together to promote human understanding.

Richard E. Mayer is a professor of psychology at the University of California, Santa Barbara. In 2000, he was recipient of the E. L. Thorndike Award for career achievement in educational psychology. Dr. Mayer is author of 12 books, including *The Promise of Educational Psychology*.

Multimedia Learning

Richard E. Mayer

University of California,
Santa Barbara

CAMBRIDGE
UNIVERSITY PRESS

PUBLISHED BY THE PRESS SYNDICATE OF THE UNIVERSITY OF CAMBRIDGE
The Pitt Building, Trumpington Street, Cambridge, United Kingdom

CAMBRIDGE UNIVERSITY PRESS
The Edinburgh Building, Cambridge CB2 2RU, UK
40 West 20th Street, New York, NY 10011-4211, USA
477 Williamstown Road, Port Melbourne, VIC 3207, Australia
Ruiz de Alarcón 13, 28014, Madrid, Spain
Dock House, The Waterfront, Cape Town 8001, South Africa

http://www.cambridge.org

First published 2001
Reprinted 2002, 2003

Printed in the United States of America

Typefaces Palatino 10/12.5 pts. *System* QuarkXPress™ [HT]

A catalogue record for this book is available from the British Library.

Library of Congress Cataloging in Publication Data

Mayer, Richard E., 1947–
    Multimedia learning / Richard E. Mayer.
        p. cm.
    Includes bibliographical references (p.) and index.
    ISBN 0-521-78239-2—ISBN 0-521-78749-1 (pb)
        1. Computer-assisted instruction. 2. Interactive multimedia. I. Title

LB1208.5 .M36 2001
371.33'467–dc21   00-041421

ISBN 0 521 78239 2 hardback
ISBN 0 521 78749 1 paperback

Dedicated to Beverly

Contents

Preface

For hundreds of years, verbal messages – such as lectures and printed lessons – have been the primary means of explaining ideas to learners. Although verbal learning offers a powerful tool for humans, this book explores ways of going beyond the purely verbal. An alternative to purely verbal presentations is to use multimedia presentations in which people learn from both words and pictures – a situation that I call *multimedia learning*. Recent advances in graphics technology have prompted new efforts to understand the potential of multimedia as a means of promoting human understanding – a potential that I call the *promise of multimedia learning*. In particular, my focus in this book is on whether people learn more deeply when ideas are expressed in words and pictures rather than in words alone.

Multimedia encyclopedias have become the latest addition to students' reference tools, and the World Wide Web is full of messages that combine words and pictures. Do these forms of presentation help learners? How do people learn from words and pictures? What is the best way to design multimedia messages? These are the kind of questions prompted by advances in graphics technology. My premise in this book is that the answers to these questions require a program of careful, systematic research. To understand how to design multimedia messages, it is useful to understand how people learn from words and pictures.

Throughout the 1990s and beyond, my colleagues and I at Santa Barbara have been conducting dozens of research studies on multimedia learning. This book provides a systematic summary of what we have found. The outcome is a set of seven principles for the design of multimedia messages and a cognitive theory of multimedia learning. In short, this book summarizes research aimed at realizing the promise of multimedia learning – that is, the potential of using words and pictures together to promote human understanding.

This book is intended for anyone who is interested in the scientific underpinnings of multimedia learning. This book could be used in courses across a university, including psychology, education, and computer science; and in specialties such as educational technology, instructional design, applied cognitive psychology, technical writing, graphic design, and human–computer interaction. I do not assume that the reader has any previous knowledge of psychology, education, or technology. I do assume that the reader is interested in the promise of multimedia learning – that is, in understanding how to tap the potential of multimedia messages for improving human understanding.

This book has both a theoretical and practical orientation. On one hand, it is aimed at those with interests in basic theory and research in the cognitive psychology of how people learn from words and pictures. On the other hand, it is aimed at those with practical interests in designing effective multimedia presentations. If your interests are in the theoretical or practical bases of multimedia learning (or a combination of the two), then this book is for you.

Writing this book has been my labor of love. I hope that you enjoy reading it as much as I have enjoyed writing it. If you have any comments or suggestions, I would like to hear from you (at mayer@psych.ucsb.edu).

ACKNOWLEDGMENTS

Much of the work reported in this book was conducted in collaboration with colleagues and students at the University of California, Santa Barbara (UCSB). I am pleased to acknowledge the substantial contributions of those with whom I have published research articles on multimedia learning: Richard B. Anderson, Dorothy Chun, Joan Gallini, Stefan Hagmann, Shannon Harp, Julie Heiser, Detlev Leutner, Roxana Moreno, Peter Nenninger, Jan Plass, and Valerie Sims. My most frequent research collaborator, Roxana Moreno, deserves special mention for her tireless efforts to conduct high-quality research on multimedia learning. I also wish to acknowledge the contributions of my faculty colleagues at UCSB who have helped me better understand the nature of multimedia learning, including Tanya Atwater, Jim Blascovich, Dorothy Chun, Mary Hegarty, Jack Loomis, Bill Prothero, Duane Sears, and Terry Smith. I appreciate the helpful comments of reviewers, including Paul Chandler, Jan Plass, Lloyd Rieber, and Wolfgang Schnotz. Although they cannot be held responsible for any failings of this book, they all deserve credit for maintaining my interest in multimedia learning. In addition, I gratefully acknowledge the contributions of Julia Hough, editor at Cambridge University Press, and Larry Meyer of Hermitage Publishing Services.

I appreciate the excellent research environment in the Department of Psychology at UCSB, as well as the opportunity to interact with a talented group of students and professors. Throughout my 25 years at UCSB, I have always enjoyed the opportunity to pursue research issues that come my way. In addition, I owe a special thanks to my mentors at the University of Michigan, including James Greeno.

I fondly acknowledge the influence of my parents, James and Bernis Mayer, who instilled in me a love of learning and helped me appreciate the indispensable value of intellectual honesty and boundless curiosity. Their memory is never far from my thoughts. I appreciate the interest of my children – Ken, Dave, and Sarah – who often asked, "How's the book doing?" They have brought much light into my life. Finally, this book would not have been possible without the encouragement and support of my wife, Beverly. I am pleased to dedicate the book to her, with love.

RICHARD E. MAYER
Santa Barbara, CA

1

The Promise of Multimedia Learning

Multimedia (as used in this book) refers to the presentation of material using both words and pictures. The case for multimedia rests in the premise that learners can better understand an explanation when it is presented in words and pictures than when it is presented in words alone. Multimedia messages can be described in terms of the delivery media (e.g., amplified speaker and computer screen), presentation mode (e.g., words and pictures), or sensory modalities (e.g., auditory and visual). The process of multimedia learning can be viewed as information acquisition (in which multimedia messages are information delivery vehicles) or as knowledge construction (in which multimedia messages are aids to sense making). Three possible learning outcomes are no learning (as indicated by poor retention and poor transfer performance), rote learning (as indicated by good retention and poor retention performance), and meaningful learning (as indicated by good retention and transfer performance). Meaningful learning outcomes depend on the cognitive activity of the learner during learning rather than on the learner's behavioral activity during learning.

▓▒ ▪ Chapter Outline

1

WHAT IS MULTIMEDIA?

The term *multimedia* means different things to different people. For some people, *multimedia* means that a person sits at a computer terminal and receives a presentation consisting of on-screen text, on-screen graphics or animation, and sounds coming from the computer's speakers – as with an on-line multimedia encyclopedia. For some people, *multimedia* means a "live" presentation in which a group of people seated in a room views images presented on one or more screens and hears music or other sounds presented via speakers. Watching a video on a TV screen can be called a multimedia experience because both images and sounds are presented. Another example of multimedia is a PowerPoint presentation in which someone presents slides from a computer projected onto a larger screen and talks about each one. Even low-tech environments allow for multimedia, such as a "chalk and talk" presentation in which someone writes or draws on a blackboard (or uses an overhead projector) while presenting a lecture. Finally, the most basic form of multimedia is a textbook lesson consisting of printed text and illustrations.

I define *multimedia* as the presentation of material using both words and pictures. By words, I mean that the material is presented in *verbal form,* such as using printed or spoken text. By pictures, I mean that the material is presented in *pictorial form,* such as using static graphics, including illustrations, graphs, photos, or maps, or using dynamic graphics, including animation or video. This definition is broad enough to cover each of the multimedia scenarios I just described, ranging from multimedia encyclopedia entries to textbook lessons. For example, in a multimedia encyclopedia, the words can be presented as on-screen text or as narration, and the pictures can be presented as graphics or animation or video. In a textbook, the words can be presented as printed text and the pictures as illustrations (or other kinds of graphics).

For purposes of conducting research, I have focused the definition of *multimedia* on just two presentation formats. Thus, the definition of multimedia I use in this book is narrower than some other definitions. A broader definition could say that multimedia is the presentation of material in more than one form. Instead, I have opted to limit the definition to just two forms – verbal and pictorial – because the research base in cognitive psychology is most relevant to this distinction. Thus, what I call multimedia learning is more accurately called dual-code or dual-channel learning.

Is *multimedia* a noun or an adjective? When used as a noun, *multimedia* refers to a technology for presenting material in both visual and verbal forms. In this sense, *multimedia* means "multimedia technology" – devices used to present visual and verbal material. When used as an adjective, *multimedia* can be used in the following contexts:

Multimedia learning – learning from words and pictures,
Multimedia message or *multimedia presentation* – presentation involving words and pictures, or
Multimedia instructional message or *multimedia instructional presentation* (or *multimedia instruction*) – presentation involving words and pictures that is intended to foster learning.

My focus in this book is on the design of multimedia instructional messages that promote multimedia learning.

In the remainder of this chapter, I present the case for multimedia learning, and then I examine three views of multimedia messages, two views of multimedia design, two metaphors of multimedia learning, three kinds of multimedia learning outcomes, and two kinds of active learning. For purposes of conducting research, I have focused on just one kind of multimedia message – instruction aimed at explaining how something works. In chapter 2, I present examples of what I call multimedia instructional messages. For purposes of conducting research, my colleagues and I have restricted our studies of multimedia learning to focus on learning from words and pictures. In chapter 3, I propose a cognitive theory of multimedia learning which explains how people learn from words and pictures. In chapters 4 through 10, I describe each of seven principles for the design of multimedia instructional messages, and in chapter 11 I summarize these principles.

THE CASE FOR MULTIMEDIA LEARNING

An instructional message is a communication that is intended to foster learning. In presenting an instructional message to learners, designers have two main formats available – words and pictures. Words include speech and printed text; pictures include static graphics (such as illustrations and photos) and dynamic graphics (such as animation and video). For hundreds of years, the major format for presenting instructional messages has been words, including lectures and books. In short, verbal modes of presentation have dominated the way we convey explanations to one another, and verbal learning has dominated education. Similarly, verbal learning has been the major focus of educational research.

The advent of computer technology has enabled an explosion in the availability of visual ways of presenting material, including large libraries of static images as well as compelling dynamic images in the form of animation and video. In light of the power of computer graphics, it may be useful to ask whether it is time to expand instructional messages beyond the purely verbal. What are the consequences of adding pictures to words? What happens when instructional messages involve both verbal and visual modes of learning? What affects the way that people learn from words and pictures? In short, how can multimedia presentations foster meaningful learning? These are the kinds of questions addressed in this book.

The case for multimedia learning is based on the idea that instructional messages should be designed in light of how the human mind works. Let's assume that humans have two information processing systems – one for verbal material and one for visual material. Let's also acknowledge that the major format for presenting instructional material is verbal. The rationale for multimedia presentations – that is, presenting material in words and pictures – is that it takes advantage of the full capacity of humans for processing information. When we present material only in the verbal mode, we are ignoring the potential contribution of our capacity to also process material in the visual mode.

Why might two channels be better than one? Two explanations are the quantitative rationale and the qualitative rationale. The quantitative rationale is that more material can be presented on two channels than on one channel – just like more traffic can travel over two lanes than one lane. In the case of explaining how a car's braking system works, for example, the steps in the process can be presented in words or can be depicted in illustrations. Presenting both is like presenting the material twice – giving the learner twice as much exposure to the explanation. Although the quantitative rationale makes sense as far as it goes, I reject it mainly because it is incomplete. In particular, I am concerned about the assumption that the verbal and visual channels are equivalent – that is, that words and pictures are simply two equivalent ways for presenting the same material.

In contrast, the qualitative rationale is that words and pictures, although qualitatively different, can complement one another and that human understanding occurs when learners are able to mentally integrate visual and verbal representations. As you can see, the qualitative rationale assumes that the two channels are not equivalent; words are useful for presenting certain kinds of material – perhaps representations that are more formal and require more effort to translate – whereas pictures are more useful for presenting other kinds of material – perhaps more intuitive, more natural representations. In short, one picture is not necessarily equivalent to 1,000 words (or any number of words).

The most intriguing aspect of the qualitative rationale is that understanding occurs when learners are able to build meaningful connections between visual and verbal representations – such as being able to see how the words *the piston moves forward in the master cylinder* relates to the forward motion of a piston in master cylinder in an animation of a car's braking system. In the process of trying to build connections between words and pictures, learners are able to create a deeper understanding than from words or pictures alone. This idea is at the heart of the cognitive theory of multimedia learning that is described in chapter 3.

THREE VIEWS OF MULTIMEDIA MESSAGES

The term *multimedia* can be viewed in three ways – based on the devices used to deliver an instructional message (i.e., the delivery media), the representational formats used to present the instructional message (i.e., the presentation modes), or the sense modalities the learner uses to receive the instructional message (i.e., sensory modalities).

The Delivery Media View

The most obvious view is that *multimedia* means the presentation of material using two or more delivery devices. The focus is on the physical system used to deliver the information – such as computer screens, amplified speakers, projectors, video recorders, blackboards, and human voice boxes. For example, in computer-based multimedia, material can be presented via the screen and via the speakers. These devices can even be broken down further by defining each window on a computer screen as a separate delivery device and each sound track coming from a speaker as a separate delivery device. In lecture-based multimedia, material can be presented via a projection on a screen and via the lecturer's voice. In the strictest interpretation of the delivery media view, a textbook does not constitute multimedia because the only presentation device is ink printed on paper.

What's wrong with this view of multimedia? Technically, it is the most accurate because it focuses on the media used to present information, but psychologically, it does more to confuse the issue than to clarify it. The emphasis is on the devices used to present information rather than on how people learn. In short, I reject the delivery media view because it focuses on technology rather than on learners.

The Presentation Modes View

A second view is that multimedia means the presentation of material using two or more presentation modes. The focus is on the way that material is represented, such as through the use of words or pictures. For example, in computer-based multimedia, material can be presented verbally as on-screen text or narration, and pictorially as static graphics or animation. In lecture-based multimedia, material can be presented verbally as speech and pictorially as projected graphics or video. In a textbook, material can be presented verbally as printed text and pictorially as static graphics.

This view is learner-centered if we assume that learners are able to use various coding systems to represent knowledge, such as verbal and pictorial knowledge representations. Although conventional wisdom is that a picture can be converted into words and vice versa, research on mental representations suggests that verbal ways of representing knowledge may be qualitatively different from pictorial ways of representing knowledge. In short, the presentation modes view of multimedia is consistent with a cognitive theory of learning, which assumes humans have separate information processing channels for verbal and pictorial knowledge. Paivio's (1986) dual-code theory presents the most coherent theoretical and empirical evidence for this idea.

The Sensory Modalities View

The third view, although also learner-centered, takes a somewhat different approach. According to the sensory modalities view, *multimedia* means that two or more sensory systems in the learner are involved. Instead of focusing on codes used to represent knowledge in learners' information processing systems, the sensory modalities view focuses on the sensory receptor the learner uses to perceive the incoming material, such as the eyes and the ears. For example, in a computer-based environment, an animation can be perceived visually and a narration can be perceived auditorially. In a lecture scenario, the speaker's voice is processed in the auditory channel and the slides from the projector are processed in the visual channel. In a textbook, illustrations and printed text are both processed visually, at least initially.

This view is learner-centered because it takes the learner's information processing activity into account. Unlike the presentation modes view, however, the sensory modalities view is that multimedia involves presenting material that is processed visually and auditorily. This distinction is based on the idea that humans process visual images and sounds in qualitatively different ways. In short, the sensory modalities view of multimedia is consistent with a cognitive theory of learning, which assumes humans have separate information processing channels for auditory and visual processing. Baddeley's (1992) model of working memory presents the most coherent theoretical and empirical evidence for this idea.

Figure 1.1 summarizes the differences among the these three views. In sum, I reject the delivery media view because it emphasizes the technology over the learner. Both the presentation modes and sensory modalities views focus on the information processing system of the learner and assume that humans process information in more than one channel – a proposal that I call the dual-channel assumption. However, they differ in the way they conceptualize the nature of the two channels: The presentation modes view distinguishes between separate systems for processing verbal and pictorial knowledge, whereas the sensory modes view distinguishes between separate systems for auditory and visual processing (i.e., for processing sounds and visual images). Although my definition of *multimedia* is based on the presentation modes view (i.e., *multimedia* means presentations using words and pictures), I also rely on the sensory modalities view (i.e., *multimedia* means

Figure 1.1   Three Views of Multimedia

View	Definition	Example
Delivery media	Two or more delivery devices	Computer screen and amplified speakers; projector and lecturer's voice
Presentation modes	Verbal and pictorial representations	On-screen text and animation; printed text and illustrations
Sensory modalities	Auditory and visual senses	Narration and animation; lecture and slides

presentations using auditory and visual material) for conceptualizing aspects of the dual channels in the human information system. A goal of the research presented in this book is to examine the relative contributions of both views of multimedia.

TWO VIEWS OF MULTIMEDIA DESIGN

Multimedia instructional messages offer a potentially powerful learning technology – that is, a system for enhancing human learning. A practical goal of research on multimedia is to devise design principles for multimedia presentations. It is useful to distinguish between two approaches to multimedia design – a technology-centered approach and a learner-centered approach.

Technology-Centered Approaches

The most straightforward approach to multimedia design is technology-centered. Technology-centered approaches begin with the functional capabilities of multimedia and ask, "How can we use these capabilities in designing multimedia presentations?" The focus is generally on cutting-edge advances in multimedia technology, so technology-centered designers might focus on how to incorporate multimedia into emerging communications technologies such as wireless access to the World Wide Web or the construction of interactive multimedia representations in virtual reality. The kinds of research issues often involve media research – that is, determining which technology is most effective for presenting information. For example, a media research issue is whether students learn as well from an on-line lecture – in which the students can see a lecturer in a window on the computer screen – as from a live lecture – in which the student is actually sitting in a classroom.

What's wrong with technology-centered approaches? A review of educational technologies of the twentieth century shows that the technology-centered approach generally fails to lead to lasting improvements in education (Cuban, 1986). For example, when the motion picture was invented in the early twentieth century, hopes were high that this visual technology would improve education. In 1922, famous inventor Thomas Edison predicted that "the motion picture is destined to revolutionize our educational system and that in a few years it will supplant largely, if not entirely, the use of textbooks" (cited in Cuban, 1986, p. 9). Like current claims for the power of visual media, Edison proclaimed that "it is possible to teach every branch of human knowledge with the motion picture" (cited in Cuban, 1986, p. 11). In spite of the grand predictions, a review of educational technology reveals that "most teachers used films infrequently in their classrooms" (Cuban, 1986, p. 17). From our vantage point beyond the close of the twentieth century, it is clear that the predicted educational revolution in which movies would replace books has failed to materialize.

Consider another disappointing example that may remind you of current claims for the educational potential of the World Wide Web. In 1932, Benjamin Darrow, founder of the Ohio School of the Air, proclaimed that radio could "bring the world to the classroom, to make universally available the services of the finest teachers, the inspiration of the greatest leaders…" (cited in Cuban, 1986, p. 19). His colleague, William Levenson, the director of the Ohio School of the Air, predicted in 1945 that a "radio receiver will be as common in the classroom as the blackboard" and that "radio instruction will be integrated into school life" (cited in Cuban, 1986, p. 19). As we rush to wire our schools and homes for access to the educational content of the Internet, it is humbling to recognize what happened to a similarly motivated movement for radio: "Radio has not been accepted as a full-fledged member of the educational community" (Cuban, 1986, p. 24).

Third, consider the sad history of educational television – a technology that combined the visual power of the motion picture with the worldwide coverage of radio. By the 1950s, educational television was touted as a way to create a "continental classroom" that would provide access to "richer education at less cost" (Cuban, 1986, p. 33). Yet, a review shows that teachers use television infrequently, if at all (Cuban, 1986).

Finally, consider the most widely acclaimed technological accomplishment of the twentieth century – computers. The technology that supports computers is different from that used in film, radio, and television, but the grand promises to revolutionize education are the same. Like current claims for the mind-enhancing power of computer technology, during the 1960s computer tutoring machines were predicted to eventually replace teachers. The first large-scale implementation occurred under the banner of computer-assisted instruction, in which computers presented short frames, solicited a response from the learner, and provided feedback to the learner. In spite of a large financial investment to support computer-assisted instruction, sound evaluations showed that the two largest computer-based systems in the 1970s – PLATO and TICCIT – failed to produce better learning than did traditional teacher-lead instruction (Cognition and Technology Group at Vanderbilt, 1996).

What can we learn from the humbling history of the twentieth century's great educational technologies? Although different technologies underlie film, radio, television, and computer-assisted instruction, they all produced the same cycle. First, they began with grand promises about how the technology would revolutionize education. Second, there was an initial rush to implement the cutting-edge technology in schools. Third, from the perspective of a few decades later, it became clear that the hopes and expectations were largely unmet.

What went wrong with these technologies that seemed poised to tap the potential of visual and worldwide learning? I attribute the disappointing results to the technology-centered approach taken by the promoters. Instead of adapting technology to fit the needs of human learners, humans were forced to adapt to the demands of cutting-edge technologies. The driving force behind the implementations was the power of the technology rather than an interest in promoting human cognition. The focus was on giving people access to the latest technology rather than helping people to learn through the aid of technology.

Are we about to replicate the cycle of high expectations, large-scale implementation, and disappointing results in the realm of multimedia technology? In my opinion, the answer to that question depends on whether we continue to take a technology-centered approach. When we ask, "What can we do with multimedia?" and when our goal is to "provide access to technology," we are taking a technology-centered approach with a 100-year history of failure.

Learner-Centered Approaches

Learner-centered approaches offer an important alternative to technology-centered approaches. Learner-centered approaches begin with an understanding of how the human mind works and ask, "How can we adapt multimedia to enhance human learning?" The focus is on using multimedia technology as an aid to human cognition. Research questions focus on the relation between design features and the human information processing system, such as comparing multimedia designs that place light versus heavy loads on the learner's visual information processing channel. The premise underlying the learner-centered approach is that multimedia designs that are consistent with the way the human mind works are more effective in fostering learning than those that are not. This premise is the central theme of chapter 3, which lays out a cognitive theory of multimedia learning.

Norman (1993, p. xi) eloquently makes the case for a learner-centered approach to technology design, which he refers to as human-centered technology: "Today we serve technology. We need to reverse the machine-centered point of view and turn it into a person-centered point of view: Technology should serve us." Consistent with the learner-centered approach, Norman (1993, p. 3) shows how "technology can make us smart" – that is, technology can expand our cognitive capabilities. Norman (1993, p. 5) refers to tools that aid the mind as *cognitive artifacts*: "Anything invented by humans for the purpose of improving thought or action counts as an artifact." Examples include mental tools such as language and arithmetic as well as physical tools such as paper and pencils; as the twentieth century's most important new cognitive artifact, computer technology represents a landmark invention that has the potential to assist human cognition in ways that were previously not possible.

Norman's (1993, p. 9) assessment is that "much of science and technology takes a machine-centered view of the design of machines" so that "the technology that is intended to aid human cognition ... more often interferes and confuses." In contrast, Norman's (1993, p. 12) vision of a learner-centered approach to technology design is that "technology ... should complement human abilities, aid those activities for which we are poorly suited, and enhance and help develop those for which we are ideally suited." The design of multimedia technology to promote human cognition represents one exemplary component in the larger task of creating what Norman (1993) calls "things that make us smart."

In his review of computer technology, Landauer (1995, p. 3) proclaims that "the computer and information revolution is widely predicted to be as consequential as the industrial revolution of the previous two centuries." Further, he describes two major phases in the use of computer technology – *automation* and *augmentation*. In the automation phase, computers are used to replace humans on certain tasks, ranging from robots in manufacturing to imaging modalities (such as computed tomography scanning and magnetic resonance imaging) in medicine to computer-based switching in telecommunications. However, Landauer (1995, p. 6) observes that the automation phase "is running out of steam" because almost all of the easy-to-automate tasks have been computerized.

The second phase of computer application – augmentation – involves the use of computers to enhance human performance on various cognitively complex tasks. Augmentation involves designing computer systems "to act as assistants, aids, and power tools" (Landauer, 1995, p. 7). However, Landauer (1995, p. 7) is disappointed with progress in the augmentation phase: "It is here ... that we have failed." A major challenge in making the augmentation phase work involves the learner-centered design of computer-based technologies: "They are still too hard to use" (Landauer, 1995, p. 7). The design of multimedia learning environments that promote meaningful human learning is an example of using computers to augment or aid human cognition – and thus one element in Landauer's augmentation phase.

The differences between the technology-centered and learner-centered approaches to multimedia design are summarized in Figure 1.2.

TWO METAPHORS OF MULTIMEDIA LEARNING

Design decisions about the use of multimedia depend on the designer's underlying conception of learning. In this section, I examine two contrasting views of multimedia learning – *multimedia learning as information acquisition* and *multimedia learning as knowledge construction*. If you view multimedia learning as information acquisition, then multimedia is an information delivery system. If you view multimedia learning as knowledge construction, then multimedia is a cognitive aid.

Multimedia Learning as Information Acquisition

According to the information acquisition view, learning involves adding information to one's memory. This view entails assumptions about the nature of what is learned, the nature of the learner, the nature of the teacher, and the goals of multimedia presentations. First, learning is based on information – an objective item that can be moved from place to place (such as from the computer screen to the human mind). Second, the learner's job is to receive information; thus, the learner is a passive being who takes in information from the outside and stores it in memory. Third, the teacher's job – or, in this case, the multimedia designer's job – is to present information. As you can see, in this view

Figure 1.2 Two Views of Multimedia Design

Design approach	Starting point	Goal	Issues
Technology-centered	Capabilities of multimedia technology	Provide access to information	How can we use cutting-edge technology in designing multimedia presentations?
Learner-centered	How the human mind works	Aid human cognition	How can we adapt multimedia technology to aid human cognition?

of learning, the responsibility for the instructional episode rests with the teacher. Thus, the information acquisition view of learning is analogous to the *information delivery* view of teaching. Fourth, the goal of multimedia presentations is to deliver information as efficiently as possible. The underlying metaphor is that of multimedia as a delivery system; according to this metaphor, multimedia is a vehicle for efficiently delivering information to the learner.

The information acquisition view is sometimes called the *empty vessel* view because the learner's mind is seen as an empty container that needs to be filled by the teacher pouring in some information. Similarly, this is sometimes called the *transmission* view because the teacher transmits information to be received by the learner. Finally, this is sometimes called the *commodity* view because information is seen as a commodity that can be moved from one place to another.

What's wrong with the information acquisition view? If your goal is to help people learn isolated fragments of information, then I suppose nothing is wrong with the information acquisition view. However, when your goal is to promote understanding of the presented material, the information acquisition view is not very helpful. Even worse, it conflicts with the research base on how people learn complex material (Bransford, Brown, & Cocking, 1999; Lambert & McCombs, 1998). When people are trying to understand presented material – such as a lesson on how a car's braking system works – they are not tape recorders who carefully store each word. Rather, humans focus on the meaning of presented material and interpret it in light of their prior knowledge.

Multimedia Learning as Knowledge Construction

In contrast, according to the knowledge construction view, multimedia learning is a sense-making activity in which the learner seeks to build a coherent mental representation from the presented material. Unlike information, which is an objective commodity that can be moved from one mind to another, knowledge is personally constructed by the learner and cannot be delivered in exact form from one mind to another. This is why two learners can be presented with the same multimedia message and come away with different learning outcomes. Second, according to the knowledge construction view, the learner's job is to make sense of the presented material; thus, the learner is an active sense maker who experiences a multimedia presentation and tries to organize and integrate the presented material into a coherent mental representation. Third, the teacher's job is to assist the learner in this sense-making process; thus, the teacher is a cognitive guide who provides needed guidance to support

Figure 1.3 Two Metaphors of Multimedia Learning

Metaphor	Definition	Content	Learner	Teacher	Goal of multimedia
Information acquisition	Adding information to memory	Information	Passive information receiver	Information provider	Deliver information; act as a delivery vehicle
Knowledge construction	Building a coherent mental structure	Knowledge	Active sense maker	Cognitive guide	Provide cognitive guidance; act as a helpful communicator

the learner's cognitive processing. As you can see, the responsibility for learning belongs to the learner, with the teacher acting as a facilitator. Fourth, the goal of multimedia presentations is not only to present information but also to provide guidance for how to process the presented information – that is, for determining what to pay attention to, how to mentally organize it, and how to relate it to prior knowledge. Finally, the guiding metaphor is that of multimedia as a helpful communicator; according to this metaphor, multimedia is a sense-making guide – that is, an aid to knowledge construction.

Figure 1.3 summarizes the differences between the two views of multimedia learning. In this book, I favor a knowledge construction view because it is more consistent with the research base on how people learn and because it is more consistent with my goal of promoting understanding of presented material. Rather than seeing the goal of multimedia presentations as exposing learners to vast quantities of information, I see the goal of multimedia as helping people develop an understanding of important aspects of the presented material. This book reflects the idea that the conception of learning has changed from being able to remember and repeat information to being able to find and use it. For example, Bransford et al. (1999, p. xi) noted that "in the last 30 years ... views of how effective learning proceeds have shifted from the benefits of diligent drill and practice to focus on students' understanding and application of knowledge." In short, the knowledge construction view offers a more useful conception of learning when the goal is to help people to understand and to be able to use what they learned.

THREE KINDS OF MULTIMEDIA LEARNING OUTCOMES

There are two major kinds of goals of learning – remembering and understanding. Remembering is the ability to reproduce or recognize the presented material and is assessed by retention tests. The most common retention tests are recall, in which learners are asked to reproduce what was presented (such as writing down all they can remember for a lesson they read), and recognition, in which learners are asked to select what was presented (as in a multiple-choice question) or judge whether a given item was presented (as in a true–false question). Thus, the major issue in retention tests involves quantity of learning – that is, how much was remembered.

Understanding occurs when learners construct a coherent mental representation from the presented material; it is reflected in the ability to use the presented material in novel situations and is assessed by transfer tests. In a transfer test, learners must solve problems that were not explicitly given in the presented material – that is, they must apply what they learned to a new situation. An example is an essay question that asks learners to generate solutions to a problem, which requires going beyond the presented material. The major issue in transfer tests involves the quality of learning – that is, how well can someone use what he or she has learned. The distinction between remembering and understanding is summarized in Figure 1.4. My goal in this book is to promote understanding as well as retention.

Consider the following scenario. Alice turns on a computer, selects an on-line multimedia encyclopedia, and clicks on the entry for "brakes." On the screen appears a passage consisting of on-screen text; it explains the steps in the operation of a car's braking system, beginning with stepping on the brake pedal and ending with the car's coming to a stop. Alice reads casually, looking at each word but hardly focusing on the material. When I ask her to explain how a car's braking system works, she performs poorly, recalling almost none of the eight steps that were presented. When I ask her to solve some problems based on the presented material, such as speculating on why a car's braking system might fail, she also performs poorly, generating almost no creative solutions (such as saying that a piston could be stuck or a brake line may have a hole in it). This is an example of a learning outcome that is all too familiar – *no learning.* In the case of no learning, the learner performs poorly on tests of retention of transfer. Alice lacks knowledge about the braking system.

Next, consider Brenda. She reads the same brakes passage as Alice but tries hard to learn the presented material. When I ask her to write an explanation of how a car's braking system works, she performs well, recalling many of the eight steps in the passage. However, when I

Figure 1.4 Two Goals of Multimedia Learning

Goal	Definition	Test	Example test item
Remembering	Ability to reproduce or recognize presented material	Retention	Write down all you can remember from the passage you just read.
Understanding	Ability to use presented material in novel situations	Transfer	List some ways to improve the reliability of the device you just read about.

ask her to solve transfer problems, she performs poorly, like Alice. This is an example of another common kind of learning outcome – *rote learning*. The distinguishing pattern for rote learning outcomes is good retention and poor transfer. In this case, Brenda has acquired what can be called *fragmented knowledge* or *inert knowledge,* knowledge that can be remembered but cannot be used in new situations. In short, Brenda has acquired a collection of *factoids* – isolated bits of information.

Finally, consider a third learner, Cathy. When she clicks on "brakes," she receives a multimedia presentation consisting of the same on-screen text that Alice and Brenda saw, as well as a computer-generated animation depicting the steps in the operation of a car's braking system. When I ask Cathy to write an explanation of how a car's braking system works, she performs well recalling as many of the steps as Brenda did. When I ask her to solve transfer problems, unlike Brenda, she performs well, generating many creative solutions. Cathy's performance suggests a third kind of learning outcome – *meaningful learning*. Meaningful learning is distinguished by good transfer performance as well as good retention performance. Presumably, Cathy's knowledge is organized into an integrated representation.

The three kinds of learning outcomes are summarized in Figure 1.5. My goal in this book is to examine design features of multimedia that foster meaningful learning. In particular, I focus on ways of integrating words and pictures that foster meaningful learning outcomes.

TWO KINDS OF ACTIVE LEARNING

What's the best way to promote meaningful learning outcomes? The answer rests in *active learning* – meaningful learning outcomes occur as a result of the learner's activity during learning. However, does *active learning* refer to what's going on with the learner's physical behavior – such as the degree of hands-on activity – or to what's going on in the learner's mind – such as the degree of integrative cognitive processing?

Figure 1.5 Three Kinds of Multimedia Learning Outcomes

		Test performance	
Learning outcome	*Cognitive description*	*Retention*	*Transfer*
No learning	No knowledge	Poor	Poor
Rote learning	Fragmented knowledge	Good	Poor
Meaningful learning	Integrated knowledge	Good	Good

In short, if the goal is to foster meaningful learning outcomes, should multimedia presentations be designed mainly to prime behavioral activity or to prime cognitive activity?

Consider the following situation: Alan is preparing for an upcoming test in meteorology. He sits in front of a computer and clicks on an interactive tutorial on lightning. The tutorial provides hands-on exercises in which he must fill in blanks by typing in words. For example, on the screen appears the following sentence: *Each year approximately _____ Americans are killed by lightning.* He types in an answer, and the computer then provides the correct answer. In this case, Alan is behaviorally active, in that he is typing answers on the keyboard, but he may not be cognitive active, in that he is not encouraged to make sense of the presented material.

In contrast, consider the case of Brian, who is also preparing for the same upcoming meteorology test. Like Alan, he sits in front of a computer and clicks on a tutorial about lightning; however, Brian's tutorial is a short narrated animation explaining the steps in the lightning formation. As he watches and listens, Brian tries to focus on the essential steps in lightning formation and to organize them into a cause-and-effect chain. Wherever the multimedia presentation is unclear about why one step leads to another, Brian uses his prior knowledge to help create an explanation for himself – which Chi, Bassok, Lewis, Reimann, and Glaser (1989) have called a *self-explanation*. For example, when the narration says that positively charged particles come to the surface of the earth, Brian mentally creates the explanation that opposite charges attract. In this scenario, Brian is behaviorally inactive because he simply sits in front of the computer; however, he is cognitively active because he is actively trying to make sense of the presentation.

Which type of active learning promotes meaningful learning? Research on learning shows that meaningful learning depends on the learner's cognitive activity during learning rather than on the learner's behavioral activity during learning. You might suppose that the best way to promote meaningful learning is through hands-on activity, such as a highly interactive multimedia program. However, behavioral activity per se does not guarantee cognitively active learning; it is possible to engage in hands-on activities that do not promote active cognitive processing, such as in the case of Alan or many highly interactive computer games. You might suppose that presenting material to a learner is not a good way to promote active learning because the learner appears to sit passively. In some situations, your intuitions would be right – presenting a long, incoherent, and boring lecture or textbook chapter is unlikely to foster meaningful learning. However, in

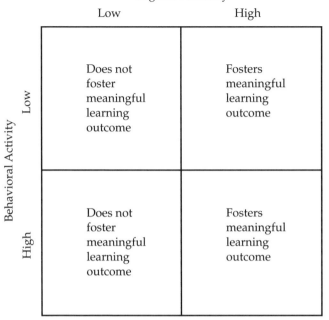

Figure 1.6 Two kinds of active learning.

other situations, such as the case of Brian, learners can achieve meaningful learning in a behaviorally inactive environment such as a multimedia instructional message. My point is that well-designed multimedia instructional messages can promote active cognitive processing in
learners, even when learners seem to be behaviorally inactive.

Figure 1.6 summarizes the two kinds of active learning – behavioral
activity and cognitive activity. If meaningful learning depends on
active cognitive processing in the learner, then it is important to design
learning experiences that prime appropriate cognitive processing. In
this book, I focus mainly on learning from multimedia instructional
messages with which learners may appear to be behaviorally inactive
but that are designed to promote active cognitive learning.

SUGGESTED READINGS

What is Multimedia?

Helander, M. G., Landauer, T. K., and Prabhu, P. V. (Eds.) (1997). *Handbook of
human-computer interaction.* Amsterdam: Elsevier.

Jonassen, D. H. (Ed.). (1996). *Handbook of research for educational communications
and technology.* New York: Macmillan.

The Case for Multimedia Learning

*Mayer, R. E. (in press). The challenge of multimedia literacy. In A. W. Pailliotet & P. B. Mosenthal (Eds.), *Reconceptualizing literacy in the new age of media, multimedia, and hypermedia.* Norwood, NJ: JAI/Ablex.

Three Views of Multimedia Messages

*Mayer, R. E. (1997). Multimedia learning: Are we asking the right questions? *Educational Psychologist, 32,* 1–19.

Two Views of Multimedia Design

Cuban, L. (1986). *Teachers and machines: The classroom use of technology since 1920.* New York: Teachers College Press.

Landauer, T. K. (1995). *The trouble with computers.* Cambridge, MA: MIT Press.

*Mayer, R. E. (1999d). Instructional technology. In F. Durso (Ed.), *Handbook of applied cognition* (pp. 551–570). Chichester, England: Wiley.

Norman, D. A. (1993). *Things that make us smart.* Reading, MA: Addison-Wesley.

Two Metaphors of Multimedia Learning

Bransford, J. D., Brown, A. L., Cocking, R. R. (Eds.). (1999). *How people learn.* Washington, DC: National Academy Press.

Lambert, N. M., & McCombs, B. L. (1998). *How students learn.* Washington, DC: American Psychological Association.

*Mayer, R. E. (1992). Cognition and instruction: Their historic meeting within educational psychology. *Journal of Educational Psychology, 84,* 405–412.

Three Kinds of Multimedia Learning Outcomes

Krathwohl, D. R., Anderson, L. W., Airasian, P. W., Mayer, R. E., Pintrich, R. E., & Raths, J. (in press). *A taxonomy of learning for teaching: A revision of Bloom's taxonomy of educational objectives.* New York: Addison-Wesley-Longman.

Mayer, R. E. (1999c). *The promise of educational psychology.* Upper Saddle River, NJ: Prentice Hall/Merrill.

Two Kinds of Active Learning

*Mayer, R. E. (1999e). Designing instruction for constructivist learning. In C. M. Reigeluth (Ed.), *Instructional design theories and models* (pp. 141–159). Mahwah, NJ: Erlbaum.

Mayer, R. E. (1993a). Problem-solving principles. In M. Fleming & W. H. Levie (Eds.), *Instructional message design: Principles from behavioral and cognitive sciences* (2nd ed., pp. 253–282). Englewood Cliffs, NJ: Educational Technology Publications.

---

* Asterisk indicates that a portion of the chapter is based on this publication.

2

Multimedia Instructional Messages

A multimedia instructional message is a communication using words and pictures that is intended to promote learning. For example, a multimedia instructional message in a book could include printed text and illustrations, whereas a multimedia instructional message on a computer could include narration and animation. Examples of multimedia instructional messages include words and pictures intended to explain how lightning storms develop, how car braking systems work, and how bicycle tire pumps work.

■■ Chapter Outline

WHAT ARE MULTIMEDIA INSTRUCTIONAL MESSAGES?

This book is concerned with the design of *multimedia instructional messages*. A multimedia instructional message is a communication using words and pictures that is intended to promote learning. This definition has three parts: First, the *message* part of the term reflects the idea that multimedia instructional messages are communications or presentations involving a teacher and learner. Second, the *instructional* part of the definition reflects the idea that the purpose of the multimedia instructional message is to promote learning (including understanding) in the learner. Third, the *multimedia* part of the definition reflects

21

the idea that the multimedia instructional message is presented using both words and pictures.

In this chapter, I present three main examples of multimedia instructional messages: an explanation of how lightning storms develop, an explanation of how car braking systems work, and an explanation of how bicycle tire pumps work. For each example, I present the explanation in words to show the conventional way the material is presented as a single-media instructional message. Then, I show how a book-based multimedia instructional message can be constructed using printed text and illustrations, and how a computer-based multimedia instructional message can be constructed using narration and animation. Finally, I show how learning can be measured by using retention tests – to see how well the learner remembers the explanation – and transfer tests – to see how well the learner understands the explanation.

HOW LIGHTNING STORMS DEVELOP

Consider the following scenario. As part of a project, you wish to find out how lightning storms develop. You look up *lightning* in an encyclopedia and come across the following entry:

Lightning can be defined as the discharge of electricity resulting from the difference in electrical charges between the cloud and the ground.

When the surface of the earth is warm, moist air near the earth's surface becomes heated and rises rapidly, producing an updraft. As the air in these updrafts cools, water vapor condenses into water droplets and forms a cloud. The cloud's top extends above the freezing level. At this altitude, the air temperature is well below freezing, so the upper portion of the cloud is composed of tiny ice crystals.

Eventually, the water droplets and ice crystals in the cloud become too large to be suspended by updrafts. As raindrops and ice crystals fall through the cloud, they drag some of the air from the cloud downward, producing downdrafts. The rising and falling air currents within the cloud may cause hailstones to form. When downdrafts strike the ground, they spread out in all directions, producing gusts of cool wind people feel just before the start of the rain.

Within the cloud, the moving air causes electrical charges to build, although scientists do not fully understand how it occurs. Most believe that the charge results from the collision of the cloud's light, rising water droplets and tiny pieces of ice against hail and other heavier, falling particles. The negatively charged particles fall to the bottom of the cloud, and most of the positively charged particles rise to the top.

The first stroke of a cloud-to-ground lightning flash is started by a stepped leader. Many scientists believe that it is triggered by a spark between the areas of positive and negative charges within the cloud. A stepped leader moves downward in steps, each of which is about 50 yards long, and lasts for about 1 millionth of a second. It pauses between steps for about 50 millionths of a second. As the stepped leader nears the ground, positively charged upward-moving leaders travel up from such objects as trees and buildings to meet the negative charges. Usually, the upward-moving leader from the tallest object is the first to meet the stepped leader and complete a path between cloud and earth. The two leaders generally meet about 165 feet above the ground. Negatively charged particles then rush from the cloud to the ground along the path created by the leaders. It is not very bright and usually has many branches.

As the stepped leader nears the ground, it induces an opposite charge, so positively charged particles from the ground rush upward along the same path. This upward motion of the current is the return stroke, and it reaches the cloud in about 70 microseconds. The return stroke produces the bright light that people notice in a flash of lightning, but the current moves so quickly that its upward motion cannot be perceived. The lightning flash usually consists of an electrical potential of hundreds of millions of volts. The air along the lightning channel is heated briefly to a very high temperature. Such intense heating causes the air to expand explosively, producing a sound wave we call thunder.

You read the words carefully, but if you are like most learners my colleagues and I have studied you may not understand the passage. In our research, students who read this 500-word passage do not perform very well on tests of retention and transfer, even when we give the tests immediately after students finish reading the passage. When we ask students to write down an explanation of how lightning storms develop (i.e., a retention test), students typically can remember fewer than half of the main steps in lightning formation. When we ask them to answer questions that require using what was presented to solve novel problems such as figuring out how to reduce the intensity of lightning storms (i.e., a transfer test), students typically are unable to generate many useful solutions. Clearly, the time-honored traditional method for presenting instructional messages – providing an explanation in the form of printed words – does not seem to work so well.

These kinds of results lead us to search for ways to make the material more understandable for students. Given our findings of the limitations of verbal forms of presentation, our search led us to the possibilities of visual forms of presentation. Can we help students understand better when we add visual representations to verbal ones? What is the best way to combine visual and verbal representations to enhance learning? These are the questions that motivate this book.

In particular, we have examined two kinds of multimedia learning situations – a book-based environment and a computer-based environment. In a book-based environment, we can focus on the issue of how best to integrate printed text and illustrations. For example, Figure 2.1 presents a book-based multimedia lesson on lightning formation – what I call *annotated illustrations*. The lesson consists of a series of illustrations, each depicting a key step in lightning formation, along with corresponding text segments (or annotations), each describing a key step in lightning formation. The five illustrations are simple line drawings containing only essential elements such as positive and negative particles, updrafts and downdrafts, and warm and cold air. The text captions also focus mainly on the essential elements and events in lightning formation; the 50 words used in the illustrations are selected verbatim from the 500 words used in the longer passage. Importantly, the illustrations and text are coordinated so that corresponding segments of text and illustrations are presented near each other on the page. We place each of these five annotated illustrations next to the corresponding paragraph in the longer 500-word passage that you just read. This is a multimedia lesson because it includes both words (i.e., printed text) and pictures (i.e., illustrations).

The annotated illustrations presented in Figure 2.1 are based on several general design principles adapted from Levin and Mayer's (1993) analysis of illustrations in text:

concentrated – The key ideas (i.e., the steps in lightning formation) are highlighted both in the illustrations and in the text.

concise – Extraneous descriptions (e.g., stories about people being struck by lightning) are minimized in the text and extraneous visual features (e.g., unneeded details or colors) are minimized in the illustrations.

correspondent – Corresponding illustrations and text segments are presented near each other on the page.

concrete – The text and illustrations are presented in ways that allow for easy visualization.

coherent – The presented material has a clear structure (e.g., a cause-and-effect chain).

comprehensible – The text and illustrations are presented in ways that are familiar and allow the learner to apply relevant past experience.

codable – Key terms used in the text and key features of the illustration are used consistently and in ways that make them more memorable.

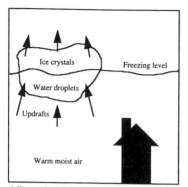

1. Warm moist air rises, water vapor condenses and forms a cloud.

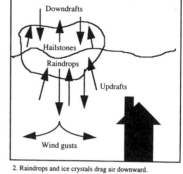

2. Raindrops and ice crystals drag air downward.

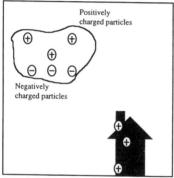

3. Negatively charged particles fall to the bottom of the cloud.

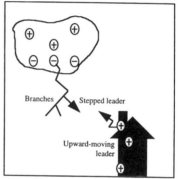

4. Two leaders meet, negatively charged particles rush from the cloud to the ground.

5. Positively charged particles from the ground rush upward along the same path.

Figure 2.1   Annotated illustrations for the book-based lightning lesson. (Figure 1 in Mayer, Bove, Bryman, Mars, & Tapangco, 1996. Copyright 1996 by the American Psychological Association. Reprinted with permission.)

In short, the annotated illustrations presented in Figure 2.1 constitute an example of a well-constructed multimedia message.

The same approach can be used to produce a multimedia lesson within a computer-based environment. Figure 2.2 presents selected frames from a computer-based multimedia lesson on lightning formation that I call a *narrated animation*. The lesson consists of a 140-second animation, depicting the key steps in lightning formation, along with a corresponding 300-word narration spoken in a male voice, describing each key step in lightning formation. The animation is adapted from the line drawings used in the illustrations, and the narration is a shortened version of the text. The animation uses simple line drawings consisting of only a few essential elements and events, and the narration also focuses on only a few essential elements and events. Importantly, the words and pictures are coordinated so that when an action takes place in the animation, there is also a verbal description of the action at the same time. In this way, the narrated animation summarized in Figure 2.2 is an example of a well-constructed multimedia message. This is a multimedia lesson because it contains both words (i.e., narration) and pictures (i.e., animation).

How can we assess what someone learns from multimedia presentations such as those depicted in Figures 2.1 and 2.2? The traditional measures of learning are retention and transfer. *Retention* refers to being able to remember what was presented. For example, the top portion of Figure 2.3 shows that as a retention test for the lightning lesson we can ask learners to write down an explanation of how lightning storms develop. In our studies, we typically allow students six minutes to write their answers for the retention test. Some of the key steps in lightning formation, based on our presentation, are these:

1. Air rises.
2. Water condenses.
3. Water and crystals fall.
4. Wind is dragged downward.
5. Negative charges fall to the bottom of the cloud.
6. The leaders meet.
7. Negative charges rush down.
8. Positive charges rush up.

I refer to these as *explanative idea units* because they are the main steps in the explanation. To compute a retention score for a learner, I can examine what the learner writes – that is, the learner's *recall protocol* – and then judge which of the eight main steps are included. In making this judgment, I focus on the meaning of the learner's answer rather

"Cool moist air moves over a warmer surface and becomes heated."

"Warmed moist air near the earth's surface rises rapidly."

"As the air in this updraft cools, water vapor condenses into water droplets and forms a cloud."

"The cloud's top extends above the freezing level, so the upper portion of the cloud is composed of tiny ice crystals."

"Eventually, the water droplets and ice crystals become too large to be suspended by the updrafts."

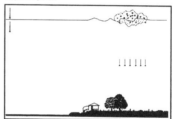

"As raindrops and ice crystals fall through the cloud, they drag some of the air in the cloud downward, producing downdrafts."

"When downdrafts strike the ground, they spread out in all directions, producing the gusts of cool wind people feel just before the start of the rain."

"Within the cloud, the rising and falling air currents cause electrical charges to build."

(Continues)

Figure 2.2 Frames from the narrated animation for the computer-based lightning lesson. (From Figure 1 in Mayer & Moreno, 1998. Copyright 1998 by the American Psychological Association. Reprinted with permission.)

"The charge results from the collision of the cloud's rising water droplets against heavier, falling pieces of ice."

"The negatively charged particles fall to the bottom of the cloud, and most of the positively charged particles rise to the top."

"A stepped leader of negative charges moves downward in a series of steps. It nears the ground."

"A positively charged leader travels up from such objects as trees and buildings."

"The two leaders generally meet about 165-feet above the ground."

"Negatively charged particles then rush from the cloud to the ground along the path created by the leaders. It is not very bright."

"As the leader stroke nears the ground, it induces an opposite charge, so positively charged particles from the ground rush upward along the same path."

"This upward motion of the current is the return stroke. It produces the bright light that people notice as a flash of lightning."

Figure 2.2   Continued

than on the exact wording. Thus, if the learner wrote "negative parts move to the cloud's bottom," the learner would get credit for idea 5 even though the wording is not exact. To make sure the scoring is objective, the recall protocol is scored by two independent scorers who do not know which instructional message the learner received. In gen-

Figure 2.3   Retention and Transfer Questions for the Lightning Lesson

Retention Test
Please write down an explanation of how lightning works.

Transfer Test
1. What could you do to decrease the intensity of lightning?
2. Suppose you see clouds in the sky but no lightning. Why not?
3. What does air temperature have to do with lightning?
4. What causes lightning?

eral, there are few disagreements, but all disagreements are resolved by consensus. Thus, the retention performance of each learner is expressed as a percentage – that is, the number of idea units remembered divided by the total possible (i.e., eight).

Although retention measures are important, I am most interested in measures of transfer. Not only do I want students to be able to remember what was presented but I also want them to be able to use what they have learned to solve problems in new situations. Thus, I did not stop with measuring how much is remembered; in fact, the main focus of my research is on measuring students' understanding by measuring their transfer performance.

The bottom portion of Figure 2.3 lists some transfer questions for the lightning lesson. The first question is a redesign question, asking the learner to modify the system to accomplish some function; the second question is a troubleshooting question, asking the learner to diagnose why the system might fail; the third question is a prediction question, asking the learner to describe the role of a particular element or event in the system; and the fourth question is a conceptual question, asking the learner to uncover an underlying principle (such as that opposite charges attract). The student is given the questions one at time on a sheet of paper and is allowed 2.5 minutes to write as many acceptable answers as possible. After 2.5 minutes, the question sheet is collected and the next question sheet is handed out. To compute a transfer score for each learner, I count how many acceptable answers the learner wrote across all the transfer questions. To help in scoring, I construct an answer key, listing the acceptable answers for each question. For example, acceptable answers for the first question about decreasing the intensity of a lightning storm include removing positive particles from the earth's surface or placing positive particles near the cloud; acceptable answers for the second question about lack of lightning include that the top of the cloud may not be above the freezing level or that no ice crystals form; acceptable answers for the third question about the role of temperature include that the earth's surface is warm and the oncoming air is cool or that the top of the cloud is above the freezing level and the bottom of the cloud is below the freezing level; acceptable answers for the fourth question about the causes of lightning include a difference in electrical charge within the cloud and a difference in air temperature within the cloud. Answers based on common knowledge, such as using a lightning rod or not standing under a tree, were not counted as acceptable answers. Students receive credit for a particular answer if they express the idea in their written answer regardless of their writing style or use of terminology. For example, students would receive credit for the fourth question if they wrote "separation of minus and plus charges in the cloud" rather than "separation of negatively charged and positively charged particles." As with the retention test, answers to the transfer test are scored by two raters who do not know which lesson the learner received. Disagreements are rare and are settled by consensus. Overall, there were twelve possible acceptable answers across the four questions, so each learner's transfer performance can be expressed as a percentage – the number of acceptable answers generated divided by the total possible (i.e., twelve).

HOW BRAKES WORK

Having explored a physical system – the process of lightning formation – let's move on to a mechanical system – the operation of a car's braking system. Suppose your car's brakes need maintenance, so you look up an article on brakes in an encyclopedia. This article explains how cable brakes work in bicycles, how hydraulic brakes work in cars, and how air brakes work in trucks. Here's what the section on hydraulic brakes says:

Hydraulic brakes use various fluids instead of levers or cables. In automobiles, the brake fluid is in chambers called cylinders. Metal tubes connect the master cylinder with wheel cylinders located near the wheels. <u>When the driver steps on the car's brake pedal, a piston moves forward inside the master cylinder. The piston forces brake fluid out of the master cylinder and through the tubes to the wheel cylinders. In the wheel cylinders, the increase in fluid pressure makes a set of smaller pistons move. These smaller pistons activate either drum or disk brakes</u>, the two types of hydraulic brakes. Most automobiles have drum brakes on the rear wheels and disk brakes on the front wheels. Drum brakes consist of a cast-iron drum and a pair of semicircular brake stops. The drum is bolted to the center of the wheel on the inside. The drum rotates with the wheel, but the shoes do not. The shoes are lined with asbestos or some other material that can withstand heat generated by friction. <u>When the brake shoes press against the drum, both the drum and wheel stop or slow down.</u>

I have added underlining to indicate the words that explain how disk brakes work; the underlining was not in the original passage.

Did you learn much from this lesson? Did this lesson make sense to you? Admittedly, the basic explanation of how disk brakes work is presented in this passage, as indicated by the words I have underlined; however, if you are like most students who read this passage in our studies, you remember less than twenty percent of the underlined material and you are not able to answer transfer questions. Apparently, people have some difficulty in learning and understanding explanations that are presented in words alone.

Let's add some illustrations to complement the words. Figure 2.4 presents a portion of the brakes passage that uses words and illustra-

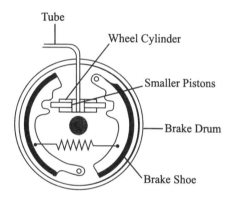

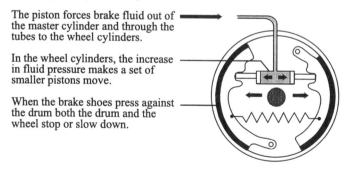

When the driver steps on the car's brake pedal...

A piston moves forward inside the master cylinder (not shown).

The piston forces brake fluid out of the master cylinder and through the tubes to the wheel cylinders.

In the wheel cylinders, the increase in fluid pressure makes a set of smaller pistons move.

When the brake shoes press against the drum both the drum and the wheel stop or slow down.

Figure 2.4 Annotated illustrations for the book-based brakes lesson. (From Figure 1 in Mayer, 1989. Copyright 1989 by the American Psychological Association. Reprinted with permission.)

tions to explain how car brakes work. The illustration shows two frames depicting the braking system – one before the driver steps on the brake pedal and one after the driver steps on the brake pedal. The illustrations are annotated with approximately seventy-five words taken from the brakes passage you just read; labels for the main parts (e.g., *tube, wheel cylinder, smaller piston, brake drum*, and *brake shoe*) and brief descriptions of each major action as underlined in the passage you read (e.g., "set of smaller pistons move"). The annotated illustrations are placed next to the corresponding paragraph in the passage; for example, the annotated illustrations about car brakes are placed next to the paragraph that covers this material. This is a book-based multimedia lesson because words are presented as printed text and pictures are presented as illustrations. I refer to the lesson in Figure 2.4 as annotated illustrations because the words and pictures are coordinated – that is, the verbal description of an event such as "set of smaller pistons move" is presented next to a visual depiction of smaller pistons moving outward.

Alternatively, let's convert the multimedia lesson on brakes into a computer-based medium consisting of animation and narration. Figure 2.5 presents selected frames from a narrated animation that explains how car brakes work. The narration, spoken in a male voice, is coordinated with the animation so that when an event is depicted in the animation (e.g., the piston's moving forward in the master cylinder) the narration concurrently describes the event in words (e.g., saying, "a piston moves forward in the master cylinder"). The presentation lasts about thirty seconds and focuses only on the essential steps in the process. The animation is based on an expanded version of the illustration in Figure 2.4 and the narration is based mainly on a slightly revised version of the underlined portion of the brakes passage you read, containing about seventy-five words. As you can see, the narrated animation focuses only on car braking systems, in contrast to the annotated illustrations, which focused on several types of braking systems.

How can we measure what a person learns from the multimedia lessons on brakes that are presented in Figures 2.4 and 2.5? As with the lightning lessons, we can measure retention – what a learner remembers from the lesson – and transfer – how well a person can apply the lesson to solving new problems. For example, the top portion of Figure 2.6 shows a simple retention test in which learners are asked to explain how car brakes work. Depending on the length of passage, I allow students five to eight minutes to write their answers for the retention test.

To measure retention, I focus on the main ideas that are presented in the part of the text that explains how car brakes work, e.g., the under-

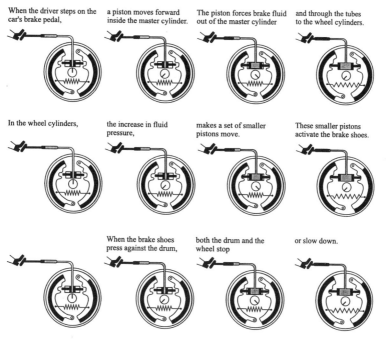

When the driver steps on the car's brake pedal, a piston moves forward inside the master cylinder. The piston forces brake fluid out of the master cylinder and through the tubes to the wheel cylinders.

In the wheel cylinders, the increase in fluid pressure, makes a set of smaller pistons move. These smaller pistons activate the brake shoes.

When the brake shoes press against the drum, both the drum and the wheel stop or slow down.

Figure 2.5 Frames from the narrated animation for the computer-based brakes lesson. (From Figure 2 in Mayer & Anderson, 1992. Copyright 1992 by the American Psychological Association. Reprinted with permission.)

Figure 2.6 Retention and Transfer Questions for the Brakes Lesson

Retention Test
1. Please write down an explanation of how a car's braking system works. Pretend that you are writing to someone who does not know much about brakes. (*Used for computer-based version*)
2. Write down all you can remember from the passage you just read. Pretend that you are writing an encyclopedia for beginners. (*Used for book-based version*)

Transfer Test
1. Why do brakes get hot?
2. What could be done to make brakes more reliable – that is, to make sure they would not fail?
3. What could be done to make brakes more effective – that is, to reduce the distance needed to bring a car to a stop?
4. Suppose you press on the brake pedal in your car but the brakes don't work. What could have gone wrong?
5. What happens when you pump the brakes (i.e., press the pedal and release the pedal repeatedly and rapidly)?

lined portion of the passage. For example, some of the key steps (which I call *explanative idea units*) for the car brakes section are these:

1. The driver steps on the brake pedal.
2. A piston moves forward inside the master cylinder.
3. A piston forces brake fluid out to the wheel cylinder.
4. Fluid pressure increases in wheel cylinders.
5. The smaller pistons move.
6. The smaller pistons activate either drum or disk brakes.
7. The brake shoes press against the drum.
8. The drum and wheel stop or slow down.

The learner's answer does not need to have the exact wording to be counted as correct. For example, if a learner writes "the shoes push on the drum," he or she would get credit for idea unit 7. I compute a percentage by counting the number of explanative idea units in the learner's answer to the retention question and dividing that by the total number of explanative idea units in the presented material.

The focus of our research is on promoting problem-solving transfer. The bottom portion of Figure 2.6 lists some transfer questions aimed at evaluating learners' understanding of how braking systems work. The first question is a conceptual question, in which the learner must uncover an underlying principle (such as the idea of friction); the second and third questions are redesign questions, in which the learner is asked to modify the system to accomplish a function; the fourth question is a troubleshooting question, in which the learner diagnoses why the system failed; and the fifth question is a prediction question, in which the learner infers what happens in the system when a certain event occurs. As in the lightning lesson, I give the learner 2.5 minutes to write as many solutions as possible for a question; the learner works on one problem at a time and is not able to go back to previous items.

For each question, I make a list of acceptable answers. For example, acceptable answers for the five questions include the following: brakes get hot because of friction (for question 1); brakes can be made more reliable by adding a backup system or a cooling mechanism (for question 2); brakes can be made more effective by using a more friction-sensitive brake shoe or by having less space between the brake shoe and brake pad (for question 3); brakes fail because there is a leak in the tube or the master cylinder is stuck in one position (for question 4); and pumping reduces heat and reduces wearing of the drum in one place (for question 5). Answers based on common knowledge, such as saying that brake shoes should be replaced regularly, are not counted as acceptable answers. I give a learner one point for each acceptable answer across all five transfer problems, using the same procedure as for the lightning lesson. Overall, there are fourteen possible acceptable answers across the five questions, so I can express each learner's transfer performance as a percentage (i.e., the number of acceptable answers the learner produced divided by the total possible).

HOW PUMPS WORK

As a third example of an instructional message, consider a passage that explains how pumps work. The passage uses words to explain several kinds of pumps, including the following excerpt explaining how a bicycle tire works:

> *Bicycle tire pumps vary in the number and location of the valves they have and in the way air enters the cylinder. Some simple bicycle tire pumps have the inlet valve on the piston and the outlet valve at the closed end of the cylinder. A bicycle tire pump has a piston that moves up and down. Air enters the pump near the point where the connecting rod passes through the cylinder. As the rod is pulled out, air passes through the piston and fills the areas between the piston and the outlet valve. As the rod is pushed in, the inlet valve closes and the piston forces air through the outlet valve.*

This paragraph seems to present plenty of worthwhile information in a clearly written way. For your information, I have underlined the portion that explains the steps in the operation of a bicycle tire pump, but this underlining is not included when we use this material in research. In spite of reading this paragraph carefully, you probably did not learn much about how pumps work. For example, students in our research studies are able to remember less than twenty-five percent of the main ideas in the passage – in this case, the underlined steps in the operation of the pump. Even worse, students who read the passage do not perform well on transfer tests in which they are asked to use the material to solve new problems; in fact, they generally fail to produce any more answers than students who do not read the passage.

These results, like those for the lightning and brake passages, led us to search for better ways to help learners understand how pumps work. The search led us beyond the domain of words to explore the potential of pictures. For example, consider the book-based multime-

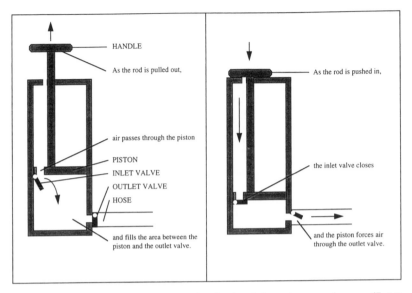

Figure 2.7 Annotated illustrations for the book-based pumps lesson. (From Figure 2 in Mayer & Gallini, 1990. Copyright 1990 by the American Psychological Association. Reprinted with permission.)

dia lesson in Figure 2.7, which uses printed text and illustrations to explain how pumps work. I refer to this lesson as annotated illustrations because it consists of words that describe the steps in how a pump works and pictures that depict the steps. The words are short sentences describing actions, such as "the inlet valve closes," and the pictures are frames depicting the pump in various states, mainly with the handle up and with the handle down. Importantly, the words and pictures are coordinated so that the verbal description of an event (such as "the inlet valve closes") is placed near a corresponding picture of the inlet valve closing. Each set of annotated illustrations is placed next to its corresponding paragraph, so that the annotated illustrations about bicycle tire pumps (shown in Figure 2.7) are placed next to the paragraph about bicycle tire pumps (shown in the box that you just read). As you can see, the words in the annotated illustrations are taken from the text passage (i.e., the underlined portion of the paragraph).

Similarly, Figure 2.8 summarizes frames from a computer-based multimedia lesson that uses animation and narration to explain how pumps work. I refer to this lesson as a narrated animation because it contains animation segments depicting steps in the operation of a pump and corresponding speech in a male voice describing the steps in words. The words and pictures are coordinated, so, for example, when the animation shows

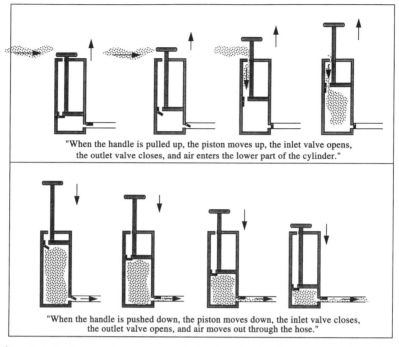

"When the handle is pulled up, the piston moves up, the inlet valve opens, the outlet valve closes, and air enters the lower part of the cylinder."

"When the handle is pushed down, the piston moves down, the inlet valve closes, the outlet valve opens, and air moves out through the hose."

Figure 2.8 Frames from the narrated animation for the computer-based pumps lesson. (From Figure 1 in Mayer & Anderson, 1991. Copyright 1991 by the American Psychological Association. Reprinted with permission.)

the inlet valve opening, the narration says, "The inlet valve opens." As you can see, the narration is modified slightly from the annotated illustrations – containing a fuller description of the steps involved in the operation of a bicycle tire pump but no extraneous details – and no other kinds of pumps are presented. The line drawing used in the animation is simple, containing only the parts mentioned in the narration, and the narration is short, containing about fifty words. The entire presentation lasts about thirty seconds.

To measure learning, I use retention and transfer tests as with the lightning and brake lessons. The top of Figure 2.9 presents a question from a retention test in which learners are asked to write down all they can remember about how pumps work. Learners are given five minutes to write an answer based on the narrated animation (which contains information about one kind of pump) and ten minutes for the annotated illustration (which contains information about three kinds of pumps). For the narrated animation, I focus on how many of the following steps (i.e. explanative idea units) about tire pumps the learner writes down:

Figure 2.9   Retention and Transfer Questions for the Pumps Lesson

Retention Test

1. Please write down an explanation of how a bicycle tire pump works. Pretend that you are writing to someone who does not know much about pumps. *(Used for computer-based version)*
2. Write down all you can remember from the passage you just read. Pretend that you are writing an encyclopedia for beginners. *(Used for book-based version)*

Transfer Test

1. What could be done to make a pump more reliable – that is, to make sure it would not fail?
2. What could be done to make a pump more effective – that is, to make it move more air more rapidly?
3. Suppose you push down and pull up the handle of a pump several times but no air comes out. What could have gone wrong?
4. Why does air enter a pump? Why does air exit from a pump?

1. The handle is pulled up.
2. The piston moves up.
3. The inlet valve opens.
4. The outlet valve closes.
5. The air enters the cylinder.
6. The handle is pushed down.
7. The piston moves down.
8. The inlet valve closes.
9. The outlet valve opens.
10. The air exits through the hose.

For the annotated illustrations, I use a similar procedure based on the steps described in the annotations. As with scoring the lightning and brakes retention tests, I compute a retention score as a percentage of the number of idea units remembered divided by the total number possible.

The bottom of Figure 2.9 contains some transfer questions. The first two questions ask the learner to redesign the system to accomplish a new function; the third question asks the learner to troubleshoot the system; and the final question asks the learner to uncover an underlying principle (i.e., air travels from high- to low-pressure areas). Acceptable answers for the first question about reliability include using airtight seals and using a backup system; acceptable answers for the second question about effectiveness include increasing the size of the cylinder or pulling harder; acceptable answers for the troubleshooting question include a hole in the cylinder and a valve stuck in one position; and acceptable answers for the last question include the idea that vacuum accounts for air entering and compression accounts for air exiting. I do not give any credit for answers based on common knowledge, such as improving reliability by using high quality components, or for vague answers, such as saying the pump doesn't work because "something is wrong with valves." On the basis of our answer key, the maximum number of points across all four transfer questions is ten, so I can compute a percentage score for each learner by dividing the number of acceptable answers by the total number possible. For both the retention and transfer test, I follow the same general scoring procedure as with lightning and brakes.

CONCLUSION

Our research focuses mainly on instructional messages involving lightning, brakes, and pumps, although the details of the instructional materials, tests, and procedure may vary from study to study. Using the same basic procedure as for lessons on lightning, brakes, and pumps, we also have examined other instructional messages, including a computer-based explanation of how a biological system works – the human respiratory system – and a book-based explanation of how a mechanical system works – the electric generator. The lesson on the human respiratory system is a forty-five second narrated animation presenting the steps in inhaling air into the lungs, exchanging oxygen and carbon dioxide between the lungs and the bloodstream, and exhaling air out of the lungs. A typical transfer question is: "Suppose you are a scientist trying to improve the human respiratory system. How could you get more oxygen into the bloodstream faster?" The lesson on electric generators is a 2,000-word passage about various types of electric generators, with sets of annotated illustrations placed next to corresponding paragraphs.

What do all these multimedia instructional messages – about lightning, brakes, pumps, lungs, and generators – have in common? First, each is a *message* – that is, a communication to a learner. In particular, I focus on a specific kind of communication, namely an explanation of how a physical, mechanical, or biological system works. Each explanation takes the form of a cause-and-effect chain in which a change in one part of the system causes a change in another part, and so on. I focus on explanations – that is, messages about cause-and-effect systems – because these are at the heart of many educational presentations on topics ranging from science to history. Second, each is *instructional* – that is, the purpose of communication is to foster learning. In particular, I measure learning through tests of retention – being able to remember the steps in the explanation – and transfer – being able to use the explanation to solve new problems. I focus on transfer because I am most interested in promoting learners' understanding of instructional messages. Third, each is based on *multimedia* because the communication is presented using both words and pictures. For book-based presentations, the words are in the form of printed text and the pictures are in the form of illustrations. For computer-based presentations, the words are in the form of narration and the pictures are in the form of animation. I focus on messages that coordinate words and pictures because I am most interested in discovering productive ways of adding pictures to words – an approach that grows from my interest in exploiting the potential of visual ways of learning.

SUGGESTED READINGS

How Lightning Storms Develop

*Mayer, R. E., Bove, W., Bryman, A., Mars, R., & Tapangco, L. (1996). When less is more: Meaningful learning from visual and verbal summaries of science texbook lessons. *Journal of Educational Psychology, 88,* 64–73.

*Levin, J. R., & Mayer, R. E. (1993). Understanding illustrations in text. In B. K. Britton, A. Woodward, & M. Binkley (Eds.), *Learning from textbooks* (pp. 95–113). Hillsdale, NJ: Erlbaum.

*Mayer, R. E., & Moreno, R. (1998). A split-attention effect in multimedia learning: Evidence for dual processing systems in working memory. *Journal of Educational Psychology, 90,* 312–320.

How Brakes Work

*Mayer, R. E. (1989). Systematic thinking fostered by illustrations in scientific text. *Journal of Educational Psychology, 81,* 240–246.

*Mayer, R. E., & Anderson, R. B. (1992). The instructive animation: Helping students build connections between words and pictures in multimedia learning. *Journal of Educational Psychology, 84,* 444–452.

How Pumps Work

*Mayer, R. E., & Anderson, R. B. (1991). Animations need narrations: An experimental test of a dual-coding hypothesis. *Journal of Educational Psychology, 83,* 484–490.

*Mayer, R. E., & Gallini, J. K. (1990). When is an illustration worth ten thousand words? *Journal of Educational Psychology, 82,* 715–726.

---

* Asterisk indicates that part of the chapter is based on this publication.

3

A Cognitive Theory
of Multimedia Learning

Multimedia messages that are designed in light of how the human mind works are more likely to lead to meaningful learning than those that are not. A cognitive theory of multimedia learning assumes that the human information processing system includes dual channels for visual/pictorial and auditory/verbal processing, that each channel has limited capacity for processing, and that active learning entails carrying out a coordinated set of cognitive processes during learning. The five steps in multimedia learning are selecting relevant words from the presented text or narration, selecting relevant images from the presented illustrations, organizing the selected words into a coherent verbal representation, organizing selected images into a coherent visual representation, and integrating the visual and verbal representations and prior knowledge. Processing of pictures occurs mainly in the visual/pictorial channel and processing of spoken words occurs mainly in the auditory/verbal channel, but processing of printed words takes place initially in the visual/pictorial channel and then moves to the auditory/verbal channel.

■■ **Chapter Outline**

The goal of this book is to examine principles for the learner-centered design of multimedia learning environments that meet three criteria: (1) *intelligibility* – the principles are derived from a cognitive theory of multimedia learning; (2) *plausibility* – the principles are consistent with empirical research on multimedia learning; (3) *applicability* – the principles can be applied to new multimedia learning situations. The second criterion, plausibility, is covered in chapters 4 through 10, which summarize an empirical research base for multimedia design principles. The third criterion, applicability, is addressed in chapter 11, which explores the applications of that research. In this chapter, I examine the first criterion by spelling out a cognitive theory of multimedia learning – that is, a cognitive theory of how people construct knowledge from words and pictures. First, I explore three fundamental assumptions underlying the theory, and second, I examine each of five steps in meaningful multimedia learning based on the theory.

THREE ASSUMPTIONS OF A COGNITIVE THEORY OF MULTIMEDIA LEARNING

According to the criterion of intelligibility, the design of multimedia environments should be compatible with how people learn. In short, principles of multimedia design should be sensitive to what we know about how people process information.

What is the role of a theory of learning in multimedia design? Decisions about how to design a multimedia message always reflect an underlying conception of how people learn, even when the underlying theory of learning is not stated. Designing multimedia messages is always informed by the designer's conception of how the human mind works.

For example, when a multimedia presentation consists of a screen over-flowing with multicolored words and images flashing and moving about, this reflects the designer's conception of human learning. The designer's underlying conception is that human learners possess a single-channel, unlimited-capacity and passive-processing system. First, by not taking advantage of auditory modes of presentation, this design is based on a single-channel assumption – that all information enters the cognitive system in the same way regardless of its modality. It follows that it does not matter which modality – such as presenting words as sounds or text – is used to present information, just as long as the information is presented. Second, by presenting so much information, this design is based on an unlimited-capacity assumption – that humans can handle an unlimited amount of material. It follows that the designer's job is to present information to the learner. Third, by presenting many isolated pieces of information, this design is based on a passive-processing assumption – that humans act as tape recorders who add as much information to their memories as possible. It follows that learners do not need any guidance in organizing and making sense of the presented information.

What's wrong with this vision of learners as possessing a single-channel, unlimited-capacity, passive processing system? Current research in cognitive psychology paints a quite different view of how the human mind works (Bransford, Brown, & Cocking, 1999; Lambert & McCombs, 1998). Thus, the difficulty with this commonsense conception of learning is that it conflicts with what is known about how people learn. In this chapter, I explore three assumptions underlying a cognitive theory of multimedia learning – *dual channels, limited capacity*, and *active processing*. These assumptions are summarized in Figure 3.1.

Figure 3.2 presents a cognitive model of multimedia learning intended to represent the human information processing system. The boxes represent memory stores, including sensory memory, working memory, and long-term memory. Pictures and words come in from the outside world as a multimedia presentation (indicated in the left side of the figure) and enter sensory memory through the eyes and ears (indicated in the **Sensory Memory** box). Sensory memory allows for pictures and printed text to be held as exact visual images for a very brief time period in a visual sensory memory (at the top) and for spoken words and other sounds to be held as exact auditory images for a very brief time period in an auditory sensory memory (at the bottom). The arrow from Pictures to Eyes corresponds to a picture being registered in the eyes; the arrow from Words to Ears corresponds to spoken text being registered in the ears; and the arrow from Words to Eyes corresponds to printed text being registered in the eyes.

Figure 3.1 Three Assumptions of a Cognitive Theory of Multimedia Learning

Assumption	Description	Related citations
Dual channels	Humans possess separate channels for processing visual and auditory information	Paivio, 1986; Baddeley, 1992
Limited capacity	Humans are limited in the amount of information that they can process in each channel at one time	Baddeley, 1992; Chandler & Sweller, 1991
Active processing	Humans engage in active learning by attending to relevant incoming information, organizing selected information into coherent mental representations, and integrating mental representations with other knowledge	Mayer, 1999c; Wittrock, 1989

The central work of multimedia learning takes place in working memory, so let's focus there. Working memory is used for temporarily holding and manipulating knowledge in active consciousness. For example, in reading this sentence, you may be able to actively concentrate on only some of the words at one time, or in looking at Figure 3.2, you may be able to hold the images of only some of the boxes and arrows in your mind at one time. This kind of processing – of which you are consciously aware – takes place in your working memory. The left side of the box labeled **Working Memory** in Figure 3.2 represents the raw material that comes into working memory – visual images of pictures and sound images of words – so it is based on the two sensory modalities that I called visual and auditory in chapter 1; in contrast, the right side of the **Working Memory** box represents the

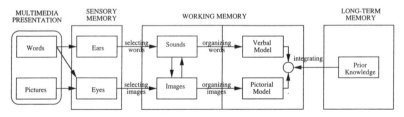

Figure 3.2 Cognitive theory of multimedia learning.

knowledge constructed in working memory – visual and verbal mental models and links between them – so it is based on the two representation modes that I called pictorial and verbal in chapter 1. The arrow from Sounds to Images represents the mental conversion of a sound (such as the spoken word *cat*) into a visual image (such as an image of a cat) – that is, when you hear the word *cat*, you might also form a mental image of a cat. The arrow from Images to Sounds represents the mental conversion of a visual image (such as a mental picture of a cat) into a sound image (such as the sound of the word *cat*) – that is, you may mentally hear the word *cat* when you see a picture of one. These processes may occur by mental association in which the spoken word *cat* primes the image of a cat and vice versa. The major cognitive processing required for multimedia learning is represented by the arrows labeled Selecting images, Selecting sounds, Organizing images, Organizing words, and Integrating, which are described in the next section.

Finally, the box on the right is labeled **Long-Term Memory** and corresponds to the learner's storehouse of knowledge. Unlike working memory, long-term memory can hold large amounts of knowledge over long periods of time, but for a person to actively think about material in long-term memory, it must be brought into working memory (as indicated by the arrow from **Long-Term Memory** to **Working Memory**).

In accord with the dual-channel assumption, I have divided **Sensory Memory** and **Working Memory** into two channels: The one across the top deals with auditory sounds and eventually with verbal representations, whereas the one across the bottom deals with visual images and eventually with pictorial representations. In this way, I try to compromise between the sensory modality view, which I use to create two channels in the left side of **Working Memory,** and the presentation mode view, which I use to create two channels on the right side of **Working Memory.** In accord with the limited-capacity assumption, working memory is limited in the amount of knowledge it can process at one time, so that only a few images can be held in the visual channel of working memory and only a few sounds can be held in the auditory channel of working memory. In accord with the active-processing assumption, I have added arrows to represent cognitive processes for selecting knowledge to be processed in working memory (i.e. arrows labeled Selecting that move from the presented material to **Working Memory**), organizing the material in working memory into coherent structures (i.e., arrows labeled Organizing that move from one kind of representation in **Working Memory** to another), and integrating the created knowledge with other knowledge, including knowledge brought in from long-term memory (i.e., arrow labeled Integrating that moves from **Long-Term Memory** to **Working Memory** and between the visual and auditory representations in **Working Memory**).

Dual-Channel Assumption

The dual-channel assumption is that humans possess separate information processing channels for visually represented material and auditorily represented material. The dual-channel assumption is summarized in Figure 3.3: Figure 3.3A shows the auditory/verbal channel highlighted and Figure 3.3B shows the visual/pictorial frame highlighted. When information is presented to the eyes (such as illustrations, animation, video, or on-screen text), humans begin by processing that information in the visual channel; when information is presented to the ears (such as narration or nonverbal sounds), humans begin by processing that information in the auditory channel. The concept of separate information processing channels has a long history in cognitive psychology and currently is most closely associated with Paivio's dual-coding theory (Clark & Paivio, 1991; Paivio, 1986) and Baddeley's model of working memory (Baddeley, 1986, 1992, 1999).

What is Processed in Each Channel?

There are two ways of conceptualizing the differences between the two channels – one based on *sensory modalities* and one based on *presentation modes*. The sensory-modality approach focuses on whether learners initially process the presented materials through their eyes (such as for pictures, video, animation, or printed words) or ears (such as for spoken words or background sounds). According to the sensory-modality approach, one channel processes visually represented material and the other channel processes auditorily represented material. This conceptualization is most consistent with Baddeley's (1986, 1992, 1999) distinction between the visuospatial sketchpad and the articulatory (or phonological) loop.

In contrast, the presentation-mode approach focuses on whether the presented stimulus is verbal (such as spoken or printed words) or nonverbal (such as pictures, video, animation, or background sounds). According to the presentation-mode approach, one channel processes verbal material and the other channel processes pictorial material and nonverbal sounds. This conceptualization is most consistent with Paivio's (1986) distinction between verbal and nonverbal systems.

Whereas the sensory-modalities approach focuses on the distinction between auditory and visual representations, the presentation-mode approach focuses on the distinction between verbal and nonverbal repre-

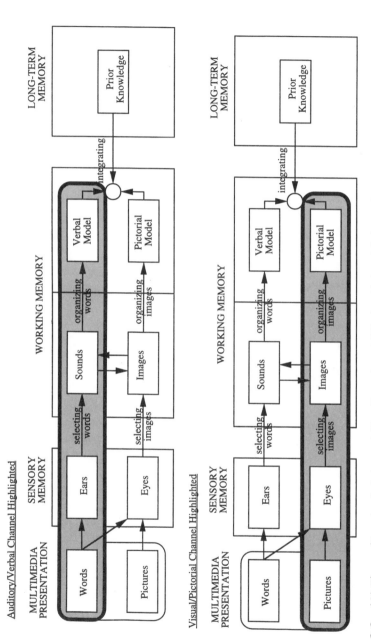

Figure 3.3 (A) The auditory/verbal channel (Top Frame) and **(B)** visual/pictorial channel (Bottom Frame) in a cognitive theory of multimedia learning.

47

sentations. The major difference concerning multimedia learning rests in the processing of printed words (i.e., on-screen text) and background sounds. On-screen text is initially processed in the verbal channel in the presentation-mode approach but in the visual channel in the sensory-modality approach; background sounds, including nonverbal music, are initially processed in the nonverbal channel in the presentation-mode approach but in the auditory channel in the sensory-mode approach.

For purposes of the cognitive theory of multimedia learning, I have opted for a compromise in which I use the sensory-modalities approach to distinguish between visually presented material (such as pictures, animation, video, and on-screen text) and auditorily pre-sented material (such as narration and background sounds) as well as a presentation-mode approach to distinguish between the construction of pictorially based and verbally based models in working memory. Thus, I distinguish between an auditory/verbal channel and a visual/pictorial channel. However, additional research is needed to clarify the nature of the differences between the two channels.

What Is the Relation between the Channels?

Although information enters the human information system via one channel, learners may also be able to convert the representation for processing in the other channel. When learners are able to devote adequate cognitive resources to the task, it is possible for information originally presented to one channel to also be represented in the other channel. For example, on-screen text may initially be processed in the visual channel because it is presented to the eyes, but an experienced reader may be able to mentally convert images into sounds that are processed through the auditory channel. Similarly, an illustration of an object or event such as a cloud's rising above the freezing level may initially be processed in the visual channel, but the learner may also be able to mentally construct the corresponding verbal descrip-tion in the auditory channel. Conversely, a narration describing some event such as "the cloud rises above the freezing level" may initially be processed in the auditory channel because it is presented to the ears, but the learner may also form a corresponding mental image that is processed in the visual channel. Such cross-channel representa-tions of the same stimulus play an important role in Paivio's (1986) dual-coding theory.

Limited-Capacity Assumption

The second assumption is that humans are limited in the amount of information that can be processed in each channel at one time. When an illustration or animation is presented, the learner is able to hold only a few images in working memory at any one time. These images reflect portions of the presented material rather than an exact copy of the presented material. For example, if an illustration or animation of a tire pump is presented, the learner may be able to focus on building mental images of the handle going down, the inlet valve opening, and air moving into the cylinder. When a narration is presented, the learner is able to hold only a few words in working memory at any one time. These words reflect portions of the presented text rather than a verbatim recording. For example, if the spoken text is "When the handle is pushed down, the piston moves down, the inlet valve opens, the outlet valve closes, and air enters the bottom of cylinder," the learner may be able to hold the following verbal representations in auditory working memory: "handle goes up," "inlet valve opens," and "air enters cylinder." The conception of limited capacity in consciousness has a long history in psychology, and some modern examples are Baddeley's (1986, 1992, 1999) theory of working memory and Chandler and Sweller's (1991; Sweller, 1999) cognitive load theory.

What Are the Limits on Cognitive Capacity?

If we assume that each channel has limited processing capacity, it is important to know just how much information can be processed in each channel. The classic way to measure someone's cognitive capacity is to give him or her a memory span test (Miller, 1956; Simon, 1974). For example, in a digit span test, I can read a list of digits at the rate of one digit per second (such as 8-7-5-3-9-6-4) and ask you to repeat them back in order. The longest list that you can recite without making an error is your memory span for digits (or digit span). Alternatively, I can show you a series of line drawings of simple objects at the rate of one per second (such as moon-pencil-comb-apple-chair-book-pig) and ask you to repeat them back in order. Again, the longest list you can recite without making an error is your memory span for pictures. Although there are individual differences, average memory span is fairly small–approximately five to seven chunks.

With practice, of course, people can learn techniques for chunking the elements in the list, such as grouping the seven digits 8-7-5-3-9-6-4 into three chunks, 875-39-64 (e.g., "eight seven five" – pause – "three nine" – pause "six four"). In this way, the cognitive capacity remains the same (e.g., five to seven chunks), but more elements can be remembered within each chunk. Researchers have developed more refined measures of verbal and visual working memory capacity but continue to show that human processing capacity is severely limited.

What Are the Sources of Cognitive Load?

Sweller and Chandler (1994) and Sweller (1999) have distinguished between intrinsic and extraneous sources of cognitive load during learning. *Intrinsic cognitive load* depends on the inherent difficulty of the material – how many elements there are and how they interact with each other. When there are many elements in the material and they are related to one another in complex ways, intrinsic cognitive load is high. In contrast, intrinsic cognitive load is low when the material is not complicated, such as when each element in the material can be learned separately. *Extraneous cognitive load* depends on the way the instructional message is designed – that is, on the way material is organized and presented. When the message is poorly designed, learners must engage in irrelevant or inefficient cognitive processing; when it is well designed, extraneous cognitive load is minimized. A goal of this book is to explore techniques for minimizing extraneous cognitive load.

How Are Limited Cognitive Resources Allocated?

The constraints on our processing capacity force us to make decisions about which pieces of incoming information to pay attention to, the degree to which we should build connections among the selected pieces of information, and the degree to which we should build connections between selected pieces of information and our existing knowledge. *Metacognitive strategies* are techniques for allocating, monitoring, coordinating, and adjusting these limited cognitive resources. These strategies are at the heart of what Baddeley (1992, 1999) has called the *central executive* – the system that controls the allocation of cognitive resources – and play a central role in modern theories of intelligence (Sternberg, 1990).

Active-Processing Assumption

The third assumption is that humans actively engage in cognitive processing to construct a coherent mental representation of their experiences. These active cognitive processes include paying attention, organizing incoming information, and integrating incoming information with other knowledge. In short, humans are active processors who seek to make sense of multimedia presentations. This view of humans as active processors conflicts with a common view of humans as passive processors who seek to add as much information as possible to memory – that is, as tape recorders who file copies of their experiences in memory to be retrieved later.

What Are the Major Ways That Knowledge Can Be Structured?

Active learning occurs when a learner applies cognitive processes to incoming material – processes that are intended to help the learner make sense of the material. The outcome of active cognitive processing is the construction of a coherent mental representation, so active learning can be viewed as a process of model building. A *mental model* (or *knowledge structure*) represents the key parts of the presented material and their relations. For example, in a multimedia presentation of how lightning storms develop, the learner may attempt to build a cause-and-effect system in which a change in one part of the system causes a change in another part. In a lesson comparing and contrasting two theories, construction of a mental model involves building a sort of matrix structure that compares the two theories along several dimensions.

If the outcome of active learning is the construction of a coherent mental representation, it is useful to explore some of the typical ways that knowledge can be structured. Some basic knowledge structures include *process, comparison, generalization, enumeration,* and *classification* (Chambliss & Calfee, 1998; Cook & Mayer, 1988). Process structures can be represented as cause-and-effect chains and consist of explanations of how some systems work. An example is an explanation of how the human ear works. Comparison structures can be represented as matrices and consist of comparisons among two or more elements along several dimensions. An example is a comparison between how two competing theories of learning view the role of the learner, the role of the teacher, and useful types of instructional methods. Generalization structures can be represented as a branching tree and consist of a main idea with subordinate supporting details. An example is a chapter outline for a chapter explaining the major causes for the American Civil War. Enumeration structures can be represented as lists and consist of a collection of items. An example is the names of principles of multimedia learning listed in this book. Classification structures can be represented as hierarchies and consist of a set and subsets. An example is a biological classification system for sea animals. These structures are summarized in Figure 3.4.

Understanding a multimedia message often involves constructing one of these kinds of knowledge structures. This assumption suggests two important implications for multimedia design: (1) the presented material should have a coherent structure and (2) the message should provide guidance to the learner for how to build the structure. If the material lacks a coherent structure, such as being a collection of isolated facts, the learner's model building efforts will be fruitless. If the message lacks guidance for how to structure the presented material,

Figure 3.4   Five Kinds of Knowledge Structures

Type of structure	Description	Representation	Example
Process	Explain a cause-and-effect chain	Flow chart	Explanation of how the human ear works
Comparison	Compare and contrast two or more elements along several dimensions	Matrix	Comparison of two theories of learning with respect to nature of the learner, teacher, and instructional methods
Generalization	Describe main idea and supporting details	Branching tree	Presentation of thesis for the major causes of the American Civil War along with evidence
Enumeration	Present a list of items	List	List of the names of seven principles of multimedia design
Classification	Analyze a domain into sets and subsets	Hierarchy	Description of a biological classification system for sea animals

the learner's model-building efforts may be overwhelmed. Multimedia design can be conceptualized as an attempt to assist learners in their model-building efforts.

What Are the Cognitive Processes Involved in Active Learning?

Three process that are essential for active learning are selecting relevant material, organizing selected material, and integrating selected material with existing knowledge (Mayer, 1996, 1999a, 1999b, 1999c; Wittrock, 1989). Selection of relevant material occurs when a learner pays attention to appropriate words and images in the presented material. This process involves bringing material from the outside into the working-memory component of the cognitive system. Organizing selected material involves building structural relations among the elements – such as one of the five kinds of structures described above. This process takes place within the working-memory component of the cognitive system. Integrating selected material with existing knowledge involves building connections between incoming material and relevant portions of prior knowledge. This process involves activating knowledge in long-term memory and bringing it into working memory. For example, in a multimedia message, learners must pay attention

Figure 3.5   Three Processes for Active Learning

Name	Description	Example
Selecting	Learner pays attention to relevant words and pictures in a multimedia message to create a word base and an image base	In viewing a narrated animation on lightning formation, learner pays attention to words and pictures describing each of the main steps
Organizing	Learner builds internal connections among selected words to create an coherent verbal model and among pictures to create a coherent pictorial model	Learner organizes the steps into a cause-and-effect chain for the words and for the pictures
Integrating	Learner builds external connections between the verbal and pictorial models and with prior knowledge	Learner makes connections between corresponding steps in the verbal chain in the pictorial chain and justifies the steps on the basis of knowledge of electricity

to certain words and images, arrange them into a cause-and-effect chain, and relate the steps to prior knowledge such as the principle that hot air rises. These processes are summarized in Figure 3.5.

In sum, the implicit theory of learning underlying some multimedia messages is that learning is a single-channel, unlimited-capacity, passive-processing activity. Thus, multimedia design is sometimes based on the empty-vessel view of learning described in chapter 1 – the idea that the learner lacks knowledge, so learning involves pouring information into the learner's empty mind. In contrast, I offer a cognitive theory of multimedia learning that is based on three assumptions about how the human mind works – namely, that the human mind is a dual-channel, limited-capacity, active-processing system.

FIVE STEPS IN A COGNITIVE THEORY OF MULTIMEDIA LEARNING

Building on the three assumptions described in the previous section, Figure 3.2 presents a cognitive theory of multimedia learning. For purposes of this book, I define a multimedia environment as one in which material is presented in more than one format, such as in words and pictures. For meaningful learning to occur in a multimedia environment, the learner must engage in five cognitive processes: (1) selecting relevant words for processing in verbal working memory, (2) selecting relevant images for processing in visual working memory, (3) organizing selected words into a verbal mental model, (4) organizing selected images into a visual mental model, and (5) integrating verbal and visual representations as well as prior knowledge. Although I present these processes as a list, they do not necessarily occur in linear order, so a learner might move from process to process in many different ways. Successful multimedia learning requires that the learner coordinate and monitor these five processes.

Selecting Relevant Words

The first labeled step listed in Figure 3.2 involves a change in knowledge representation from a sensory representation of spoken sounds entering the ears to an internal representation of word sounds in working memory. The input for this step is a spoken verbal message that is received in the learner's ears. The output for this step is a word sound base – a mental representation in the learner's verbal working memory of selected words or phrases.

The cognitive process mediating this change is called *selecting relevant words* and involves paying attention to some of the words that are presented in the multimedia message as they pass through auditory sensory memory. If the words are presented as speech, this process begins in the auditory channel (as indicated by the arrow from Words to Ears to Sounds). However, if the words are presented as on-screen text or printed text, this process begins in the visual channel (as indicated by the arrows from Words to Eyes) and later may move to the auditory channel if the learner mentally articulates the printed words (as indicated by the arrow from Images to Sounds in the left side of **Working Memory**). The need for selecting only part of the presented message occurs because of capacity limitations in each channel of the cognitive system. If the capacity were unlimited, there would be no need to focus attention on only part of the verbal message. Finally, the selection of words is not arbitrary; the learner must determine which words are most relevant – an activity that is consistent with the view of the learner as an active sense maker.

For example, in the lightning lesson, one segment of the multimedia presentation contains the words "Cool moist air moves over a warmer surface and becomes heated," the next segment contains the words "Warmed moist air near the earth's surface rises rapidly," and the next segment has the words "As the air in this updraft cools, water vapor condenses into water droplets and forms a cloud." When a learner engages in the selection process, the result may be that some of the words are represented in verbal working memory – such as "Cool air becomes heated, rises, forms a cloud."

Selecting Relevant Images

The second step involves a change in knowledge representation from a sensory representation of unanalyzed visual stimulation entering the eyes to an internal representation of visual images in working memory. The input for this step is a pictorial portion of a multimedia message that is held briefly in visual sensory memory. The output for this step is a visual image base – a mental representation in the learner's working memory of selected images.

The cognitive process underlying this change is called *selecting relevant images* and involves paying attention to part of the animation or illustrations presented in the multimedia message. It is represented by the arrow from Eyes to Images. This process begins in the visual channel, but it is possible to convert part of it to the auditory channel (such as by mentally narrating an ongoing animation). The need to select only part of the presented pictorial material arises from the limited processing capacity of the cognitive system. It is not possible to process all parts of a complex illustration or animation segment, so learners must focus on only part of the incoming pictorial material. Finally, the selection process for images – like the selection process for words – is not arbitrary because the learner must judge which images are most relevant for making sense of the multimedia presentation.

In the lightning lesson, for example, one segment of the animation shows blue arrows (but no arrows are colored in this book) – representing cool air – moving over a heated land surface that contains a house and trees; another segment shows the arrows turning red and traveling upward above a tree; and a third segment shows the arrows changing into a cloud with lots of dots inside. In selecting relevant images, the learner may compress all this into images of a blue arrow pointing rightward, a red arrow pointing upward, and a cloud; details such as the house and tree on the surface, the wavy form of the arrows, and the dots in the cloud are lost.

Organizing Selected Words

Once the learner has formed a word sound base from the incoming words of a segment of the multimedia message, the next step is to organize the words into a coherent representation – a knowledge structure that I call a *verbal model*. The input for this step is the word sound base – the words and phrases selected from the incoming verbal message – and the output for this step is a verbal model – a coherent (or structured) representation in the learner's working memory of the selected words or phrases.

The cognitive process involved in this change is *organizing selected words*, in which the learner builds connections among pieces of verbal knowledge. It is represented by the arrow from Sounds to Verbal Model. This process is most likely to occur in the auditory channel and is subject to the same capacity limitations that affect the selection process. Learners do not have unlimited capacity to build all possible connections, so they must focus on building a simple structure. The organizing process is not arbitrary but rather reflects an effort at sense making – such as the construction of a cause-and-effect chain.

For example, in the lightning lesson, the learner may build causal connections between the selected verbal components: "First, cool air is heated; second, it rises; third, it forms a cloud." In mentally building a causal chain, the learner is organizing the selected words.

Organizing Selected Images

The process for organizing images parallels that for selecting words. Once the learner has formed an image base from the incoming pictures of a segment of the multimedia message, the next step is to organize the images into a coherent representation – a knowledge structure that I call a *pictorial model*. The input for this step is the image base – the pictures selected from the incoming pictorial message – and the output for this step is a pictorial model – a coherent (or structured) representation in the learner's working memory of the selected images.

This change from images to a pictorial model requires the application of a cognitive process that I call *organizing selected images*. It is represented by the arrow from Images to Pictorial Model. In this process, the learner builds connections among pieces of pictorial knowledge. This process occurs in the visual channel, which is subject to the same capacity limitations that affect the selection process. Learners lack the capacity to build all possible connections among images in their image base and rather must focus on building a simple set of connections. As in the process of organizing words, the process of organizing images is not arbitrary. Rather, it reflects an effort at building a simple structure that makes sense to the learner, such as the cause-and-effect chain.

For example, in the lightning lesson, the learner may build causal connections between the selected images: The rightward-moving blue arrow turns into a rising red arrow, which turns into a cloud. In short, the learner builds causal links in which the first event leads to the second, and so on.

Integrating Word-Based and Image-Based Representations

Perhaps the most crucial step in multimedia learning involves making connections between word-based and image-based representations. This step involves a change from having two separate representations – a visual model and a verbal model – to having an integrated representation in which corresponding elements and relations from one model are mapped onto the other. The input for this step is the visual model and the verbal model that the learner has constructed so far, and the output is an integrated model, which is based on connecting the two representations. In addition, the integrated model includes connections with prior knowledge.

I refer to this cognitive process as *integrating* because it involves building connections between corresponding portions of the pictorial and verbal models as well as relevant existing knowledge from long-term memory. This process occurs in visual and verbal working memory and involves the coordination between them. It is represented by the arrows from the Verbal Model and the Pictorial Model as well as the arrow from **Long-Term Memory.** This is an extremely demanding process that requires the efficient use of cognitive capacity. The process reflects the epitome of sense making because the learner must focus on the underlying structure of the visual and verbal representations. The learner can use prior knowledge to help coordinate the integration process, as indicated by the arrow from **Long-Term Memory** to **Working Memory.**

For example, in the lightning lesson, the learner must see the connection between the verbal chain – "First, cool air is heated; second, it rises; third, it forms a cloud" – and the visual chain – the blue arrow followed by the red arrow followed by the cloud shape. In addition, prior knowledge can be applied to the transition from the first to the second event by remembering that hot air rises.

Each of the five steps in multimedia learning is likely to occur many times throughout a multimedia presentation. The steps are applied segment by segment, not to the entire message as a whole. For example, in processing the lightning lesson, learners do not first select all relevant words and images from the entire passage, then organize them into verbal and visual models of the entire passage, and then connect the completed models with one another at the very end. Rather, learners carry out this procedure on small segments: They select relevant words and images from the first sentence of the narration and the first few seconds of the animation; they organize and integrate them; and then this set of processes is repeated for the next segment, and so on.

In short, multimedia learning takes place within the learner's information processing system – a system that contains separate channels for visual and verbal processing, a system with serious limitations on the capacity of each channel, and a system that requires coordinated cognitive processing in each channel for active learning to occur. In particular, multimedia learning is a demanding process that requires selecting relevant words and images, organizing them into coherent verbal and pictorial representations, and integrating the verbal and pictorial representations. The theme of this book is that multimedia messages should be designed to facilitate multimedia learning processes. Multimedia messages that are designed in light of how the human mind works are more likely to lead to meaningful learning than those that are not. This proposition is tested empirically in the following seven chapters.

EXAMPLES OF HOW THREE KINDS OF PRESENTED MATERIALS ARE PROCESSED

Let's take a closer look at how three kinds of presented materials are processed from start to finish according to the model of multimedia learning summarized in Figure 3.2: pictures, spoken words, and printed words. For example, suppose that Albert clicks on an entry for *lightning* in a multimedia encyclopedia and is presented with a static picture of a lightning storm with a paragraph of on-screen text about the number of injuries and deaths caused by lightning each year. Similarly, suppose that Barbara clicks on the entry for *lightning* in another multimedia encyclopedia and is presented with a short animation along with narration describing the steps in lightning formation. In these examples, Albert's presentation contains static pictures and printed words, whereas Barbara's presentation contains dynamic pictures and spoken words.

Processing of Pictures

Figure 3.6A shows the path for processing of pictures, indicated by thick arrows and darkened boxes. The first event, represented by the Pictures box under **Multimedia Presentation** on the left side of the figure, is the presentation of Albert's lightning photograph (i.e., a static picture) or Barbara's lightning animation (i.e., a dynamic picture). The second event,

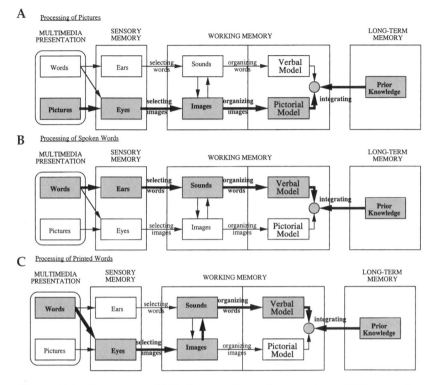

Figure 3.6 Processing of **(A)** pictures, **(B)** spoken words, and **(C)** printed words in a cognitive theory of multimedia learning.

represented by the Eyes box under **Sensory Memory,** is that the pictures impinge on the eyes, resulting in a brief sensory image; that is, for a brief time, Albert's sensory memory beholds the photograph and Barbara's sensory system beholds the animation frames. These first two events happen without much effort on the part of the learner, but now, the active cognitive processing begins – the processing over which the learner has some conscious control. If Albert pays attention to the fleeting image coming through his eyes (or Barbara attends to images coming through her eyes), parts of the image will become represented in working memory as a visual image base; this attentional processing corresponds to the arrow labeled Selecting images, and the resulting mental representation is labeled Images under **Working Memory.** The next active cognitive processing involves organizing those piecemeal images into a coherent structure, a process indicated by the Organizing images arrow. The resulting knowledge representation is a Pictorial Model. Thus, Albert builds an organized visual representation of the main parts of a lightning bolt or Barbara builds an organized set of images representing the cause-and-effect steps in lightning formation. Finally, active cognitive processing is required to connect the new representation with other knowledge, a process indicated by the Integrating arrow. For example, Albert may use his prior knowledge about electricity to help him include moving positive and negative charges in his mental representation or Barbara may use her prior knowledge of electricity to help explain why the negative and positive charges are attracted to one another. In addition, if the learners have also produced a verbal model, they may try to connect it to the pictorial model, such as looking for how a phrase in the text corresponds to a part of the image. This processing results in an integrated learning outcome, indicated by the circle under **Working Memory.**

Processing of Spoken Words

Figure 3.6B shows the path for processing of spoken words, indicated by thick arrows and darkened boxes. When the computer produces spoken narration (as indicated by the Words box under **Multimedia Presentation**), the sounds first reach Barbara's ears (as indicated by the Ears box under **Sensory Memory**). For example, when the computer says, "The negatively charged particles fall to the bottom of the cloud and most of the positively charged particles rise to the top," these words are picked up by Barbara's ears and held temporarily in her auditory sensory memory. Next, active cognitive processing can take place. If she pays attention to the sounds coming into her ears (as indicated by the arrow labeled Selecting words), some of the incoming sounds will be selected for inclusion in Barbara's word sound base (indicated by the Sounds box under **Working Memory**). For example, the resulting collection of words in working memory might include "positive top, negative bottom." The words in the word sound base are disorganized fragments, so the next step, indicated by the Organizing words arrow, is to build them into a coherent mental structure, indicated by the Verbal Model box. In this process, the words change from being represented on the basis of sound to being represented on the basis of word meaning; the result could be a cause–effect chain for the steps in lightning formation. Lastly, Barbara may use her prior knowledge to help explain the transition from one step to another and may connect words with pictures, such as connecting "positive top, negative bottom" with an image of positive particles in the top of a cloud and negative charges in the bottom. This process is labeled Integrating and the resulting integrated learning outcome is indicated by the circle under **Working Memory.**

Processing of Printed Words

So far, cognitive processing of pictures takes place mainly in the bottom channel of Figure 3.6C – that is, in the visual/pictorial channel – whereas the cognitive processing of spoken words takes place mainly in the top channel – that is, in the auditory/verbal channel. However, the arrow from the visual image base to the word sound base indicates that the learner (such as Barbara) can mentally create sounds corresponding to the visual image – such as mentally saying "wind" when she sees wavy arrows in the animation. Similarly, the arrow from the word sound base to the visual image base indicates that the learner (such as Barbara) can mentally create images corresponding to the word sound base – such as visualizing a plus sign when the narration says "positively charged particle."

The presentation of printed text in multimedia messages tends to create an information processing challenge for the dual-channel system portrayed in Figure 3.6. For example, consider the case of Alan, who must read text and view an illustration. The words are presented visually so they must initially be processed through the eyes, as indicated by the arrow from Words to Eyes. Then, Alan may attend to some of the incoming words (as indicated by the Selecting images arrow) and bring them into working memory as part of the visual image base. Then, by mentally pronouncing the images of the printed words, Alan can get the words into the word sound base (as indicated by the arrow from Images to Sounds). Once the words are represented in the auditory/verbal channel, they are processed like the spoken words, as described above. This path is presented in Figure 3.6C. As you can see, when verbal material must enter through the visual channel, the words must take a complex route through the system and must also compete for attention with the illustration that Alan is also processing via the visual channel. The consequences of this problem are addressed in more detail in chapter 8, which concerns the modality principle.

CONCLUSION

The theme of this chapter is that the design of multimedia messages should be based on a satisfactory theory of how people learn and, in particular, on a cognitive theory of multimedia learning. In this chapter, I present a cognitive theory of multimedia learning based on three well-established ideas in cognitive science – what I call the dual-channel, limited-capacity, and active processing assumptions. I show how multimedia learning occurs when the learner engages in five kinds of processing – selecting words, selecting images, organizing words, organizing images, and integrating. Finally, I give examples of how pictures, spoken words, and printed words are processed according to the cognitive theory of multimedia learning. I used this model to suggest design principles that my colleagues and I tested; this research is laid out in the next seven chapters.

SUGGESTED READINGS

There Assumptions of a Cognitive Theory of Multimedia Learning

Baddeley, A. D. (1986). *Working memory.* Oxford, England: Oxford University Press.

Baddeley, A. D. (1999). *Human memory.* Boston: Allyn & Bacon.

Chandler, P., & Sweller, J. (1991). Cognitive load theory and the format of instruction. *Cognition and Instruction, 8,* 293–332.

Clark, J. M., & Paivio, A. (1991). Dual coding theory and education. *Educational Psychology Review, 3,* 149–210.

* Mayer, R. E. (1996). Learning strategies for making sense out of expository text: The SOI model for guiding three cognitive processes in knowledge construction. *Educational Psychology Review, 8,* 357–371.

Paivio, A. (1986). *Mental representations: A dual coding approach.* Oxford, England: Oxford University Press.

Five Steps in a Cognitive Theory of Multimedia Learning and Examples of How Three Kinds of Presented Materials Are Processed

* Mayer, R. E. (1999a). Multimedia aids to problem-solving transfer. *International Journal of Educational Research, 31,* 611–623.

* Mayer, R. E. (1999b). Research-based principles for the design of instructional messages. *Document Design, 1,* 7–20.

---

* Asterisk indicates that a portion of this chapter is based on this publication.

4
Multimedia Principle

Multimedia Principle: *Students learn better from words and pictures than from words alone.*

Theoretical Rationale: *When words and pictures are both presented, students have an opportunity to construct verbal and pictorial mental models and to build connections between them. When words alone are presented, students have an opportunity to build a verbal mental model but are less likely to build a pictorial mental model and make connections between the verbal and pictorial mental models.*

Empirical Rationale: *In six of nine tests, learners who received text and illustrations or narration and animation performed better on retention tests than did learners who received text alone or narration alone. In nine of nine tests, learners who received text and illustrations or narration and animation performed better on transfer tests than did learners who received text alone or narration alone.*

■■ Chapter Outline

INTRODUCTION
Does Multimedia Work?
Are Pictures Different from Words?
Words and Pictures Are Informationally Equivalent: The Case for
Presenting Words Only
Words and Pictures Are Qualitatively Different: The Case for
Adding Pictures to Words
Distinction between Multimedia Effects and Media Effects
RESEARCH ON MULTIMEDIA
Multimedia Effect for Retention
Multimedia Effect for Transfer
Related Research on Multimedia

INTRODUCTION

Does Multimedia Work?

The first question to ask concerns whether multimedia works: Do students learn better when a lesson is presented in two or more formats than when it is presented in one? In this book, I focus on a straightforward version of this question: Do students learn better when a lesson is presented in words and pictures than when it is presented solely in words? In short, does adding pictures to a verbal lesson help students learn better?

To answer this question, it is useful to define what is meant by *lesson, words, pictures,* and *learn better.* A lesson is a presentation that is intended to foster learning in a student; in our studies, the lessons are brief explanations of how some physical, mechanical, or biological system works. By *words,* I mean printed or spoken text; in our studies, the words are short passages or narrations adapted from encyclopedias or science textbooks. By *pictures,* I mean any form of static or dynamic graphic, including photos, graphs, charts, illustrations, video, and animation; in our studies, the pictures are illustrations (consisting of two or more frames of line drawings) or animations. I use the term *learn better* to refer to improvements in retention and understanding of the presented material; in our studies, retention is measured by retention tests in which the student is asked to write down an explanation, and understanding is measured by transfer tests in which the student is asked to generate creative solutions to novel problems related to the lesson. As you can see, by using the term *learn better,* I do not mean the same as "learn more." Instead of focusing on the quantitative question of "how much is learned," I am most interested in the qualitative question of "what is learned." In particular, by focusing on transfer (in addition to retention), I can examine whether multimedia presentations improve student understanding.

The multimedia question is an important preliminary question. If the answer is no – that is, that multimedia presentations do not result in better learning than do single-medium presentations – then it is not necessary to conduct more in-depth studies. We would be able to stop this book with this chapter. If the answer is yes – that is, that multimedia presentations result in better learning than do single-medium presentations – then it is worthwhile to conduct in-depth studies. In particular, we would want to add chapters that focus on the conditions under which multimedia presentations foster meaningful learning.

Are Pictures Different from Words?

Consider the following description of how a bicycle tire pump works:

> As the rod is pulled out, air passes through the piston and fills the area between the piston and the outlet valve. As the rod is pushed in, the inlet valve closes and the piston forces air through the outlet valve.

These sentences provide a very brief and concise summary of the cause-and-effect chain involved in the operation of a tire pump: Pulling out the rod causes air to pass through the piston and fill the area between the piston and the outlet valve; pushing the rod in causes the inlet valve to close and the piston to force air through the outlet valve.

Now, examine Figure 4.1, which shows a pictorial version of this cause-and-effect chain, consisting of two line drawings. In the first frame, the rod is up and air is passing through the piston into the area between the piston and the outlet valve. In the second frame, the rod is pushed in, the inlet valve is closed, the piston has moved down, and air is moving out through the outlet valve.

Do you think that the words convey the same basic information as the picture? Do you learn the same thing from reading the two sentences as from viewing the two frames of the illustration? In short, are the two modes of presentation – words and pictures – informationally equivalent? According to the information-delivery view, the answer is yes because words and pictures are simply two different vehicles for presenting the same information. According to the cognitive theory of multimedia learning, the answer is no because words and pictures prime two qualitatively different knowledge representation systems in learners – a verbal channel and a visual channel. We explore these two views in the following two sections.

Words and Pictures Are Informationally Equivalent: The Case for Presenting Words Only

The information delivery view is that different presentation formats, such as words and pictures, are vehicles for presenting the same information.

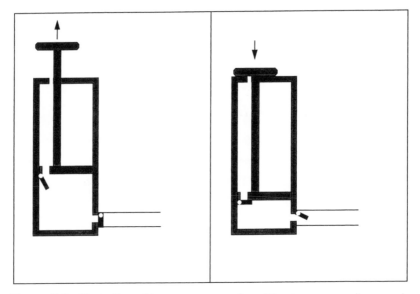

Figure 4.1   Illustration of how a pump works, without corresponding words.

A basic premise of this view is that information is an objective commodity that can be transported from the outside world to inside the human mind. This delivery can be made by words or by pictures, but the result is the same – information is stored in that great warehouse we call human memory. Thus, the words presented in the box in the previous section convey information on how a tire pump works; the picture in Figure 4.1 conveys the same information and therefore adds nothing new.

According to a strict interpretation of this view, multimedia presentations are not needed because the same information is delivered twice. Consider what happens when pumps are explained both in words and pictures. The presented words allow the learner to add the information to his or her memory, so a cause-and-effect chain is added to memory. The pictures allow the learner to add the same information to memory, but the information is redundant with what has already been delivered using words. Thus, the pictures are not needed because they add no new information beyond what has already been delivered by words.

The argument for words-only presentation is straightforward. Words are the most common way of presenting information because verbal messages are efficient and easy to create. If the learner receives the verbal message – the word-based delivery of information – then a pictorial message that delivers the same information is a waste of effort. Once a learner has received information in one format, it is a waste of effort to deliver the same information again in a different format.

In the information-delivery view, the teacher's role is to deliver information and the learner's role is to store it in memory. As long as the information is delivered, the instructor's job is done, so the instructor need only present a complete verbal explanation. Thus, a book author need not include illustrations that repeat the information in the text; a computer-based instructional designer need not include animations that repeat the information already presented as on-screen text or narration.

According to the strict interpretation of the information delivery view, students who receive presentations in words should perform as well on retention and transfer tests as students who receive presentations in words and pictures – as long as the delivery of words is fully received by the learner. This is the prediction I make for the information-delivery view in this chapter.

In contrast to this strict interpretation of the information-delivery view, a more lenient interpretation is explored in chapters 9 and 10. According to this lenient view, if a delivery route is fully or partially blocked, then multimedia presentations – that is, multiple deliveries – may result in more learning. For example, some delivery routes may be blocked when learners prefer one mode of presentation over another or have better ability in using one mode rather than another. Predictions based on this lenient interpretation of the information-delivery view are developed in chapters 9 and 10.

Words and Pictures Are Qualitatively Different: The Case for Adding Pictures to Words

The cognitive theory of multimedia learning (as described in chapter 3) is based on the idea that humans possess two qualitatively different channels for processing material – one for visually based representations and one for verbally based representations. A premise underlying this view is that pictorial mental representations and verbal mental representations are qualitatively different; by their natures, visual and verbal representations cannot be informationally equivalent.

This premise can be summarized by saying that words and pictures are two qualitatively different systems for representing knowledge. On one hand, language is one of the most important cognitive tools ever invented by humans. By using words, we can describe material in an interpreted or abstracted manner that requires some mental effort to translate. Text consists of discrete units presented in a linear sequence. On the other hand, pictures are probably the original mode of knowledge representation in humans. By using pictures, we can depict material in a form that is more intuitive and closer to our visual sensory experience. Pictures allow holistic, nonlinear representations of information. Although the same material can be described in words and depicted in pictures, the resulting verbal and pictorial representations are not informationally equivalent. Although the verbal and pictorial representations may complement one another, they cannot be substituted for one another.

The instructor's job is not only to present material but also to help guide the learner's cognitive processing of the presented material. In particular, learners are expected to build verbal and pictorial representations and to build connections between them. Carefully designed multimedia messages can foster these processes in learners.

According to the cognitive theory of multimedia learning, multimedia presentations have the potential to result in deeper learning and understanding than do presentations that are presented solely in one format. For example, Figure 4.2 shows what happens when we combine words and corresponding pictures to produce a multimedia message. The cognitive theory of multimedia learning predicts that students will learn more deeply from a multimedia message such as in Figure 4.2 than from a presentation only in one format – such as presenting only the words or only the drawings. Thus, students who learn with words and pictures should perform better on transfer tests than do students who learn only with words.

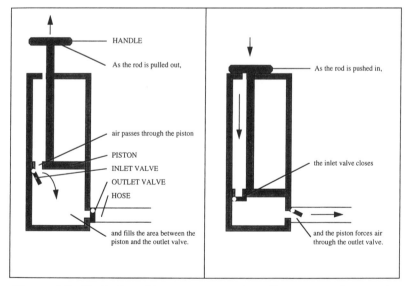

Figure 4.2 Illustration of how a pump works, with corresponding words.

The rationale for this prediction is that a multimedia presentation guides the learner to build a verbal mental model of the pump system, to build a pictorial mental model of the pump system, and to build connections between the two. The multimedia presentation allows learners to hold corresponding verbal and pictorial representations in working memory at the same time, thus increasing the chances that learners will be able to build mental connections between them. According to the cognitive theory of multimedia learning, the act of building connections between verbal and pictorial mental models is an important step in conceptual understanding; therefore, students who receive well-constructed multimedia messages should perform better on transfer tests – which are designed to measure understanding – than do students who receive messages presented only in words.

What does the cognitive theory of multimedia learning predict about retention? The retention test used in our studies is purely word based: Students are asked to write down an explanation of how a tire pump works, for example. On one hand, it is possible that students given only words could perform as well as students given words and pictures. This is so because both groups receive the same verbal explanation and then are asked to reproduce it. On the other hand, by connecting the words to the pictures, students in the multimedia group are able to create a more meaningful representation, which presumably includes all of the essential steps in the cause-and-effect explanation. This representation could help students in their recall of each of the essential steps in the causal chain, which is what we measure on the retention test. Therefore, I tentatively predict that students given words and pictures will perform better on retention tests than will students given only words.

Distinction between Multimedia Effects and Media Effects

It is useful to make a distinction between multimedia effects and media effects. The research question for multimedia effects concerns whether students learn more deeply when material is presented using two presentation forms – such as words and pictures – rather than one – such as words alone. In short, we can ask, "Are words and pictures more effective than words alone?" In contrast, the research question for media effects concerns whether students learn more deeply when material is presented via one medium – such as computer-based animation and narration – than another medium – such as book-based illustrations and text. In short, we can ask, "Are computers more effective than textbooks?"

In the debate on media effects, one side argues that media per se have little or no effect on learning (Clark, 1994), whereas the other side argues that certain media have unique potential to improve learning (Kozma, 1994). For example, suppose students learn Newtonian mechanics better in a computer-based environment than in a standard instructional environment, as reported by Kozma (1994). These results seem to support those who argue that the instructional medium can have a unique effect on learning. Yet those who hold the opposing view – that media don't affect learning – can reply by saying that it is not possible to separate the effects of the medium from the effects of the instructional method (Clark, 1994). The computer-based environment used one instructional method, whereas the conventional classroom environment used a different instructional method, so the differences may be attributable to instructional method rather than medium.

Media scholars have come to the conclusion that it is not productive to continue with traditional media research, in which one medium is compared to another (Clark, 1983; Clark & Salomon, 1986; Salomon, 1994; Wetzel, Radtke, & Stern, 1994). Media research can be criticized on empirical, methodological, conceptual, and theoretical grounds. First, media research has a somewhat disappointing history, with inconclusive empirical results (Clark & Salomon, 1986; Mayer, 1997). Although our goal was not to examine media effects in our research, I decided to reanalyze our studies to look at every possible comparison between learning from computers and learning from textbooks. Consistent with prior research on media effects, I found no substantive differences on test performance for students who received an explanation presented via animation and narration versus students who received an explanation of the same system using illustrations and text (Mayer, 1997).

Second, as demonstrated in our own comparisons, there are serious methodological confounds in comparing learning from two media. In our comparisons, for example, the tone of voice of the speaker and the way words were stressed in the narration for the computer-based presentation are different from the way that printed text was formatted into paragraphs and laid out on the page for the book-based presentation. Similarly, in some versions of the computer-based presentation, students could repeat the presentation, whereas in the text-based presentation, students had a certain time limit within which to study the text and illustrations. In short, it is not possible to determine whether differences in what students learn from text-based versus computer-based presentations are caused by the medium or by the content and study conditions, which are inseparable from the medium.

On the conceptual side, a third problem with media research is that learning depends on the quality of instructional message rather than the medium per se. It is possible to design a textbook so that students have great difficulty in understanding the material, and it is possible to design a textbook so that students can understand the presented material more easily. Similarly, it is possible to design a computer-based presentation in ways that either hinder or promote meaningful learning. Importantly, our research has shown that the same factors that improve student understanding in a book-based environment also promote student understanding in computer-based environment – such as adding pictures to words (this chapter), placing text close to corresponding graphics (chapter 5), and eliminating extraneous material (chapter 7). In both media, ineffective instructional messages can be converted into effective ones by applying the same instructional design principles (Fleming & Levie, 1993).

The fourth problem with media research concerns the theory that underlies it. Research on media effects is based on an information-delivery view of learning, in which media are delivery systems for carrying information from teacher to learner. By asking "Which medium is more effective in delivering information?" media researchers adopt the information-delivery view of learning. Jonassen and Reeves (1996, p. 693) made the point this way: "Whether one sides with those who believe that media have little or no effects on learning or those who promote its unique instructional effectiveness, such arguments are limited by narrow definitions of media as conveyors of information.... [This perspective is] inherently flawed because it fails to recognize learners as active constructors of knowledge."

The debate over media effects is based on an outmoded conception of learning that conflicts with the cognitive theory of multimedia learning and with several key ideas in cognitive psychology, including the ideas of dual-channel processing, limited capacity, and active processing. In contrast, the cognitive theory of multimedia learning, which I described in chapter 3, is based on a knowledge-construction view in which learners actively build mental representations in an attempt to make sense of their experiences. Instead of asking which medium makes the best deliveries, we might ask which instructional techniques help guide the learner's cognitive processing of the presented material.

In summary, the consensus among educational psychologists is that questions about which medium is best are somewhat unproductive questions. The rationale is empirical (in general, media effects are small), methodological (it is not possible to separate the effects of medium from the effects of instructional method), conceptual (learning outcomes depend on the quality of the instructional method rather than on the medium per se), and theoretical (learning involves knowledge construction rather than information delivery). For example,

Clark (1994) has shown how media effects can never be separated from method effects; Jonassen, Campbell, and Davidson (1994) have argued for research that focuses on how instructional treatments affect cognitive processing in the learner rather than on the effects of media per se; and Kozma (1994) has called for research on the ways that instructional methods within a medium interact with cognitive and social processes in learners. In short, Kozma (1994, p. 13) reflects the consensus "to shift the focus of our research from media as conveyors of methods to media and methods as facilitators of knowledge construction and meaning making on the part of learners." In the remainder of this chapter – and, indeed, throughout this book – we focus on how to design multimedia presentations that foster understanding in learners rather than on which medium is best.

RESEARCH ON MULTIMEDIA

Are two presentational formats better than one? Is it better to present words and pictures rather than words alone? We addressed this question in nine separate tests in which we compared the retention and transfer performance of students who received a narrated animation on pumps or brakes to the performance of students who received narration alone (Mayer & Anderson, 1991, Experiment 2a; Mayer & Anderson, 1992, Experiments 1 and 2); or we compared the retention and transfer performance of students who received text with illustrations on pumps, brakes, generators, or lightning to the performance of students who received text alone (Mayer, 1989b, Experiments 1 and 2; Mayer, Bove, Bryman, Mars, & Tapangco, 1996, Experiment 2; Mayer & Gallini, 1990, Experiments 1, 2, and 3). Figure 4.2 provides an example of the kind of material we presented to students who received both words and pictures (which I call the multiple-representation group); in contrast, the text in Figure 4.2 constitutes an example of what would be presented to students who received words alone (which I call the single-representation group). The retention test involved writing down an explanation of how the presented system works within a time limit generally of 5 to 6 minutes. The transfer test involved writing answers to problem-solving questions, generally with a 2.5-minute time limit for each question. The retention score is based on the number of main ideas that the student wrote down on the retention test; the transfer score is based on the number of creative solutions generated across all of the problem-solving transfer questions. According to the cognitive theory of multimedia learning, the multiple-representation group should outperform the single-representation group, whereas there should be no difference between the multiple- and single-representation groups according to the information-delivery theory.

Multimedia Effect for Retention

Figure 4.3 shows the mean retention scores for students who received words alone (single-representation group) and for students who received words and pictures (multiple-representation group). In six of nine experimental tests, multiple-representation learners recalled more of the steps in the causal explanation than did single-representation learners, in spite of the fact that both groups received identical verbal explanations. This pattern constitutes a *multimedia effect for retention* because adding pictures to words tended to improve student performance on retention tests. The multimedia effect for retention is that students perform better on verbal retention when they learn with text and illustrations or narration and animation than when they learn with text

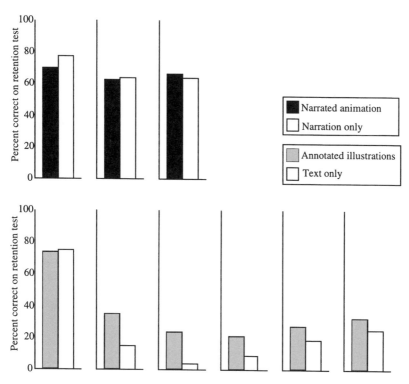

Figure 4.3 Multimedia effect for retention: better retention when words and pictures are presented (*dark bars*) rather than words alone (*white bars*).

Figure 4.4   Multimedia Effect for Retention: Summary of Results

Source	Content	Context	Effect size	Percent gain
Mayer and Anderson, 1992, Exp. 1	Pumps	Screen	−.48	−12
Mayer and Anderson, 1992, Exp. 2	Brakes	Screen	−.09	−2
Mayer and Anderson, 1991, Exp. 2a	Pumps	Screen	.13	5
Mayer et al., 1996, Exp. 2	Lightning	Page	−.07	−2
Mayer and Gallini, 1990, Exp. 1	Brakes	Page	1.33	133
Mayer and Gallini, 1990, Exp. 2	Pumps	Page	1.33	667
Mayer and Gallini, 1990, Exp. 3	Generators	Page	1.00	133
Mayer, 1989b, Exp. 1	Brakes	Page	.90	47
Mayer, 1989, Exp. 2	Brakes	Page	.67	23
Median			**.67**	**23**

alone or narration alone. Figure 4.4 shows that the effect sizes for this multimedia effect are moderate, with a median of .67. Also shown in Figure 4.4, the median improvement in retention attributable to inclusion of pictures is 23%, that is, students in the multiple-representation group produced 23% more of the steps in the causal chain than did students in the single-representation group.

Although the prediction of the cognitive theory of multimedia learning is upheld by the general pattern of results, there are some interesting contradictions. Most importantly, there was no multimedia effect in three of the nine tests and there was only a small effect in a fourth test. In particular, Figures 4.3 and 4.4 show that adding animation to narration did not help retention, whereas in general, adding illustrations to printed text did result in improved retention. One possible explanation is that the retention test involved only verbal recall; for each comparison between multiple- and single-representation groups, all learners received the same verbal explanation, so adding pictorial material might not have been important in all circumstances.

The verbal material was somewhat richer in the computer-based presentations, so it is possible that learners could build a verbal mental model from only the narration. This would explain why a multimedia effect for retention was not obtained in two of the three computer-based tests (indicated as "screen" context in Figure 4.4). The verbal material was somewhat more terse in the textbook-based presentations, so it is possible that the pictorial presentations helped fill in gaps or clarify aspects of the printed text. This would explain why a multimedia effect for retention was obtained in five of the six textbook-based tests (indicated as "page" context in Figure 4.4).

Overall, the results are inconsistent with the information-delivery theory and, in most cases, the results are consistent with the cognitive theory of multimedia learning. Further research is needed to determine the conditions under which a words-only presentation results in a high level of verbal retention.

Multimedia Effect for Transfer

The main focus of our research is on problem-solving transfer, because transfer performance is a reflection of how well students understand an instructional message. Figure 4.5 shows the mean transfer scores for students who received words and pictures (multiple-representations group) and for students who received words only (single-representation group) for each of nine experimental comparisons. In each comparison, the multiple-representations group performed better than the single-representation group on the transfer test. This can be called a *multimedia effect for transfer* because adding pictures to words resulted in improvements in students' understanding of the explanation. In sum, the multimedia effect for transfer is that students perform better

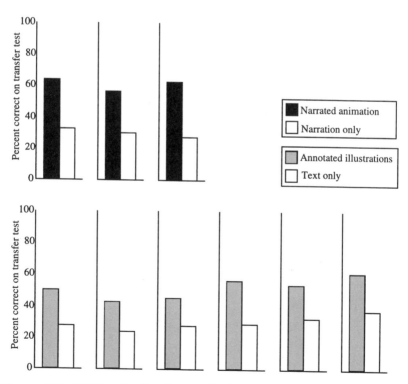

Figure 4.5 Multimedia effect for transfer: better transfer when words and pictures are presented (*dark bars*) rather than words alone (*white bars*).

on problem-solving transfer when they learn with words and pictures rather than when they learn with words alone. Figure 4.6 shows the effect size and percent gain for each of the nine comparisons. As you can see, the effect sizes are large and consistent, with a median of 1.50. This means that students who learned with words and pictures generated considerably more creative answers to problems than did students who learned with words alone – on average, the multiple-representation group generated 1.5 standard deviations more solutions than did the single-representation group. As you can also see in Figure 4.6, the percent gains are large and consistent, with a median of 89%. This means that students who learned with words and pictures generated 89% more creative solutions in the transfer test than did the students who learned with words alone.

Overall, these results are inconsistent with the information-delivery theory, which predicted no differences between the two groups, but these results are consistent with the cognitive theory of multimedia learning, which predicted that adding pictures to words would greatly enhance the understandability of an explanation.

Related Research on Multimedia

Graphics play an important role in both book-based and computer-based instruction but often are not used in a way that fosters learning. For example, in an analysis of how space is used in sixth-grade science textbooks, I found that about half of the page space was devoted to illustrations and about half was devoted to words (Mayer, 1993b). On the basis of a taxonomy developed by Levin (Levin & Mayer, 1993), I categorized each illustration as belonging to one of the following categories:

Figure 4.6 Multimedia Effect for Transfer: Summary of Results

Source	Content	Context	Effect size	Percent gain
Mayer and Anderson, 1992, Exp. 1	Pumps	Screen	1.90	96
Mayer and Anderson, 1992, Exp. 2	Brakes	Screen	1.67	97
Mayer and Anderson, 1991, Exp. 2a	Pumps	Screen	2.43	121
Mayer et al., 1996, Exp. 2	Lightning	Page	1.39	79
Mayer and Gallini, 1990, Exp. 1	Brakes	Page	1.19	79
Mayer and Gallini, 1990, Exp. 2	Pumps	Page	1.00	68
Mayer and Gallini, 1990, Exp. 3	Generators	Page	1.35	93
Mayer, 1989b, Exp. 1	Brakes	Page	1.50	89
Mayer, 1989b, Exp. 2	Brakes	Page	1.71	64
Median			**1.50**	**89**

decorative – illustrations that are intended to interest or entertain the reader but that do not enhance the message of the passage, such as a picture of a group of children playing in a park for a lesson on physics principles

representational – illustrations that portray a single element, such as a picture of the space shuttle with the heading "The Space Shuttle"

organizational – illustrations that depict relations along elements, such as a map or chart showing the main parts of the heart

explanative – illustrations that explain how a system works, such as the frames explaining how pumps work in Figure 4.2

The results were that the overwhelming majority of illustrations served no important instructional purpose: 23% were decorational and 62% were representational. In contrast, only a small minority of the illustrations enhanced the instructional message: 5% were organizational and 10% were explanative. From this kind of analysis, I conclude that the potential power of graphics is not being met.

Similarly, in an analysis of fifth-grade mathematics textbooks, my colleagues and I found that about 30% of the space was used for illustrations, but again, the majority of the illustrations were irrelevant to the goal of the lesson (Mayer, Sims, & Tajika, 1995). For example, in a section on positive and negative numbers, one book had a full-color picture of a golfer teeing off. The text went on to talk about being above and below par in a golf game. As with my analysis of science textbooks, this analysis of mathematics textbooks shows that the authors are not maximizing the potential power of graphics to enhance human learning.

Research on *graphic advance organizers* offers an important line of research that complements research on the multimedia effect. A graphic advance organizer is material – usually involving a combination of graphics and text – that is presented before a text passage and that is intended to foster understanding of the text. Because the graphic advance organizer is intended to foster understanding, I have referred to graphic advance organizers as *models for understanding* (Mayer, 1989a). In particular, the organizer is intended to prime relevant prior knowledge in the learner – including both visual and verbal knowledge structures – that the learner can integrate with the incoming text.

For example, in one study, students listened to a short passage about how radar works and later took retention and transfer tests (Mayer, 1983). For the retention test, students were asked to write down all they could remember from the passage; for the transfer test, students were asked to write answers for problems that required creative solutions such as inventing a way to increase the area under surveillance for radar. Some students were asked to study a graphic advance organizer for sixty seconds before listening to the passage. The graphic advance organizer was a sheet of paper containing five labeled line drawings showing a pulse traveling from an antenna (transmission), a pulse bouncing off an aircraft (reflection), a pulse returning to the receiver (reception), measuring the difference between "time out" and "time back" on a clock (measurement), and converting time to a measure of distance (conversion). The drawings were intended to prime the learner's prior knowledge with bouncing balls. Students who received the graphic advance organizer recalled 50% more of the conceptual material on the retention test and generated 80% more useful solutions on the transfer test than did students who did not receive the graphic advance organizer. Similar results were obtained in more than a dozen additional tests involving lessons on topics such as Ohm's law, the nitrogen cycle, and how a camera works (Mayer, 1989a).

Overall, research on illustrations in text yields two important results relevant to the multimedia effect: (1) textbook authors who add illustrations to their text often fail to take full advantage of the potential power of graphics as an aid to understanding, and (2) adding a carefully designed graphic advance organizer to a text passage can greatly enhance student understanding. Thus, this pioneering line of research on illustrations in text is consistent with what we have found in this chapter concerning the multimedia effect – adding certain kinds of pictures to words can help students to understand the instructional message. Our research on the multimedia effect is also consistent with Rieber's (1990a) finding that, under certain conditions, students learned better from a computer-based science lesson on the laws of motion when animated graphics were included.

IMPLICATIONS

Implications for Multimedia Learning

The research summarized in this chapter has shown that multimedia works – that is, at least in the case of scientific explanations, adding illustrations to text or adding animation to narration can help students to better understand the presented explanation. We refer to this result as a *multimedia effect*: Presenting an explanation with words and pictures results in better learning than does presenting words alone.

The results clearly contradict the commonsense notion that the main goal of instructional messages is to present information. We call this idea the information-delivery theory because it is based on the premise that instructional messages are vehicles for delivering information to the learner. According to this view, if information is presented in the form of words, then presenting the same information in pictures adds nothing to student learning. The results overwhelmingly contradict the prediction that students given only words will perform as well as students given words and pictures and thus cast doubt on a strict interpretation of the information-delivery theory.

The results are consistent with the cognitive theory of multimedia learning that was presented in chapter 3. In particular, the results support the idea that humans process pictures versus words using qualitatively different mental representations. A central premise is that meaningful learning occurs when learners build picture-based and word-based representations and build systematic connections between them. These cognitive processes are primed by the multiple-representation treatment, in which words and corresponding pictures are presented to learners. In contrast, presenting information in only words may encourage learners to build a word-based representation but does not prime learners to build a picture-based representation or to build systematic connections between word-based and picture-based representations. Some learners may be able to do this – by forming their own mental images based on the presented words – but the opportunities for meaningful learning are greater for the multiple-representation group. In short, our results support the thesis that a deeper kind of learning occurs when learners are able to integrate pictorial and verbal representations of the same message. Rather than adding information to memory, learners are actively constructing pictorial and verbal mental models and trying to see how they relate to one another.

Implications for Multimedia Design

The multimedia effect demonstrates that student learning can be enhanced when pictures are added to words – that is when material is presented in two forms rather than one. However, all multimedia messages are not equally effective. For example, Schnotz, Bannert, and Seufert (in press) reported situations in which some learners reduced the amount of attention they paid to text when pictures were added. The task in the remainder of this book is to pinpoint the conditions under which multimedia presentations are effective. In short, we want to know how to design multimedia messages to maximize student understanding of the presented material.

We can begin with our first principle of multimedia design: Present words and pictures rather than words alone. This multimedia principle, however, is somewhat vague and needs to be clarified. What kind of pictures should be added, how should they be added, and when should they be added? These are the kinds of clarifying issues that I address in the remaining chapters in this book. Thus, although the multimedia principle is a good starting place, it must be used in conjunction with other clarifying principles described in the following chapters.

SUGGESTED READINGS

*Mayer, R. E. (1989). Systematic thinking fostered by illustrations in scientific text. *Journal of Educational Psychology, 81,* 240–246.

*Mayer, R. E., & Anderson, R. B. (1991). Animations need narrations: An experimental test of a dual-coding hypothesis. *Journal of Educational Psychology, 83,* 484–490.

*Mayer, R. E., & Anderson, R. B. (1992). The instructive animation: Helping students build connections between words and pictures in multimedia learning. *Journal of Educational Psychology, 84,* 444–452.

*Mayer, R. E., Bove, W., Bryman, A., Mars, R., & Tapangco, L. (1996). When less is more: Meaningful learning from visual and verbal summaries of science textbook lessons. *Journal of Educational Psychology, 88,* 64–73.

*Mayer, R. E., & Gallini, J. K. (1990). When is an illustration worth ten thousand words? *Journal of Educational Psychology, 82,* 715–726.

---

* Asterisk indicates that part of the chapter is based on this publication.

5

Spatial Contiguity Principle

Spatial Contiguity Principle: Students learn better when corresponding words and pictures are presented near rather than far from each other on the page or screen.

Theoretical Rationale: When corresponding words and pictures are near each other on the page or screen, learners do not have to use cognitive resources to visually search the page or screen and learners are more likely to be able to hold them both in working memory at the same time. When corresponding words and pictures are far from each other on the page or screen, learners have to use cognitive resources to visually search the page or screen for corresponding words and pictures. Thus, learners are less likely to be able to hold them both in working memory at the same time.

Empirical Rationale: In two of two tests, learners performed better on retention tests when corresponding text and illustrations were placed near each other on the page (or when corresponding on-screen text and animation segments were placed near each other on the screen) than when they were placed far away from each other. In five of five tests, learners performed better on transfer tests when corresponding text and illustrations were placed near each other on the page (or when corresponding on-screen text and animation segments were placed near each other on the screen) than when they were placed far away from each other.

■ ■ Chapter Outline

INTRODUCTION

Space as an Economic Resource

When it comes to presenting multimedia material – words and pictures – on a computer screen or textbook page, the amount of available space is limited. A screen or page can hold only a finite amount of verbal/written or visual material. Therefore, screen space or page space can be viewed as a limited resource that is in great demand. Decisions about multimedia design can be viewed as economic decisions concerning how to allocate space on a page or screen among alternative uses. For example, my analysis of science textbooks has shown that about half the space in textbooks is used for graphics and about half is used for words (Mayer, 1993b).

In addition to deciding how much space to allocate to words and how much to allocate to pictures, multimedia designers need to determine how to arrange the word-dominated space and the picture-dominated space on the available pages or screen frames. Suppose, for example, that you had a passage on lightning formation that contained 550 words and 5 illustrations. Further, suppose that the space you have for presenting this material is two pages of paper.

On the one hand, you could place all the words on one page and all the illustrations on another page, as is shown in Figure 5.1. This is an example of a separation design because your strategy is to place graphics in a different place than text.

On the other hand, you could place each illustration next to the paragraph that describes it. To provide even better integration, you could copy some of the key words from the paragraph as a caption for the corresponding illustration. This does not add any new words but simply places the most relevant words very close to the corresponding illustration. Figure 5.2 shows an integrated way to present words and illustrations. This is an example of an integration design

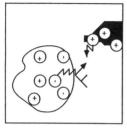
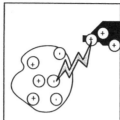
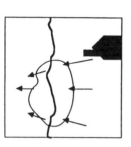
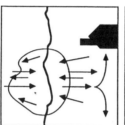
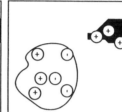
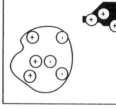

The Process of Lightning

Lightning can be defined as the discharge of electricity resulting from the difference in electrical charges between the cloud and the ground.

Warm moist air near the earth's surface rises rapidly. As the air in this updraft cools, water vapor condenses into water droplets and forms a cloud. The cloud's top extends above the freezing level. At this altitude, the air temperature is well below freezing, so the upper portion of the cloud is composed of tiny ice crystals.

Eventually, the water droplets and ice crystals become tolarge to be suspended by updrafts.

As raindrops and ice crystals fall through the cloud, they drag some of the air in the cloud downward, producing downdrafts. The rising and falling air currents within the cloud may cause hailstones to form. When downdrafts strike the ground, they spread out in all directions, producing gusts of cool wind people feel just before the start of the rain.

Within the cloud, the moving air causes electrical charges to build, although scientists do not fully understand how it occurs. Most believe that the charge results from the collision of the cloud's light, rising water droplets and tiny pieces of ice against hail and other heavier, falling particles. The negatively charged particles fall to the bottom of the cloud, and most of the positively charged particles rise to the top.

The first stroke of a flash of ground-to-cloud lightning is started by a stepped leader. Many scientists believe that it is triggered by a spark between the areas of positive and negative charges. A stepped leader moves downward in a series of steps, each of which is about 50 yards long and lasts for about 1 millionth of a second. It pauses between steps for about 50 millionths of a second. As the stepped leader nears the ground, positively charged upward-moving leaders travel up from such objects as trees and buildings to meet the negative charges. Usually, the upward-moving leader from the tallest object is the first to meet the stepped leader and complete a path between the cloud and earth. The two leaders generally meet about 165 feet above the ground. Negatively charged particles then rush from the cloud to the ground along the path created by the leaders. It is not very bright and usually has many branches.

As the leader stroke nears the ground, it induces an opposite charge, so positively charged particles from the ground rush upward along the same path. This upward motion of the current is the return stroke and it reaches the cloud in about 70 microseconds. A return stroke produces the bright light that people notice in a flash of lightning, but the current travels so quickly that its upward motion cannot be perceived. The lightning flash usually consists of an electrical potential of several million volts. The air along the lightning channel is heated briefly to a very high temperature. Such intense heating causes the air to expand explosively, producing a sound wave we call thunder.

A flash of lightning may end after one return stroke. In most cases, however, dart leaders which are similar to stepped leaders, carry more negative charges from the cloud down the main path of the previous stroke. Each dart leader is followed by a return stroke. This process commonly occurs 3 or 4 times in one flash, but can occur more than 20 times. People can sometimes see the individual strokes of a flash. At such times the lightning appears to flicker.

Figure 5.1 Separated book-based multimedia presentation: words separated from pictures.

The Process of Lightning

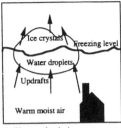

Lightning can be defined as the discharge of electricity resulting from the difference in electrical charges between the cloud and the ground.

Warm moist air near the earth's surface rises rapidly. As the air in this updraft cools, water vapor condenses into water droplets and forms a cloud. The cloud's top extends above the freezing level. At this altitude, the air temperature is well below freezing, so the upper portion of the cloud is composed of tiny ice crystals.

1. Warm moist air rises, water vapor condenses and forms cloud.

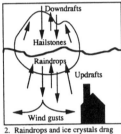

Eventually, the water droplets and ice crystals become too large to be suspended by updrafts. As raindrops and ice crystals fall through the cloud, they drag some of the air in the cloud downward, producing downdrafts. The rising and falling air currents within the cloud may cause hailstones to form. When downdrafts strike the ground, they spread out in all directions, producing gusts of cool wind people feel just before the start of the rain.

2. Raindrops and ice crystals drag air downward.

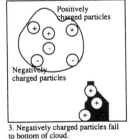

Within the cloud, the moving air causes electrical charges to build, although scientists do not fully understand how it occurs. Most believe that the charge results from the collision of the cloud's light, rising water droplets and tiny pieces of ice against hail and other heavier, falling particles. The negatively charged particles fall to the bottom of the cloud, and most of the positively charged particles rise to the top.

3. Negatively charged particles fall to bottom of cloud.

(continues)

Figure 5.2 Integrated book-based multimedia presentation: words integrated with pictures.

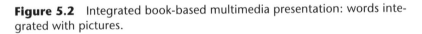

because your strategy is to place graphics close to the words that describe them.

As you can see, the multimedia lessons in Figure 5.1 and Figure 5.2 contain the same illustrations and the same words and both require two pages of space. The major difference between the two multimedia lessons is that in the first one, the words and illustrations are separated from one another on the pages and in the second one, the words and illustrations are integrated with one another on the pages.

Suppose, instead, that you have a 140-second animation depicting the formation of lightning – based on animating the illustrations from

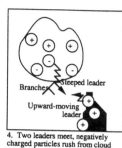

The first stoke of a flash of ground-to-cloud lightning is started by a stepped leader. Many scientists believe that it is triggered by a spark between the areas of positive and negative charges. A stepped leader moves downward in a series of steps, each of which is about 50 yards long and lasts for about 1 millionth of a second. It pauses between steps for about 50 millionths of a second. As the stepped leader nears the ground, positively charged upward-moving leaders travel up from such objects as trees and buildings to meet the negative charges. Usually, the upward-moving leader from the tallest object is the first to meet the stepped leader and complete a path between the cloud and earth. The two leaders generally meet about 165 feet above the ground. Negatively charged particles then rush from the cloud to the ground along the path created by the leaders. It is not very bright and usually has many branches.

4. Two leaders meet, negatively charged particles rush from cloud to ground.

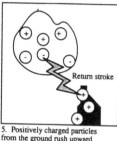

As the leader stroke nears the ground, it induces an opposite charge, so positively charged particles from the ground rush upward along the same path. This upward motion of the current is the return stroke and it reaches the cloud in about 70 microseconds. A return stroke produces the bright light that people notice in a flash of lightning, but the current travels so quickly that its upward motion cannot be perceived. The lightning flash usually consists of an electrical potential of several million volts. The air along the lightning channel is heated briefly to a very high temperature. Such intense heating causes the air to expand explosively, producing a sound wave we call thunder.

A flash of lightning may end after one return stroke. In most cases, however, dart leaders which are similar to stepped leaders, carry more negative charges from the cloud down the main path of the previous stroke. Each dart leader is followed by a return stroke. This process commonly occurs 3 or 4 times in one flash, but can occur more than 20 times. People can sometimes see the individual strokes of a flash. At such times the lightning appears to flicker.

5. Positively charged particles from the ground rush upward along the same path.

Figure 5.2 Continued.

Figures 5.1 and 5.2 – and you have about 300 words of on-screen text – based on shortening the text from Figures 5.1 and 5.2. The animation depicts about sixteen actions (such as cool, moist air moving over the earth's surface) and the text describes the same sixteen actions. How should you present the animation and text on the computer screen?

If you followed a separation strategy, you might place the text describing an action in a different place from the corresponding animation segment. For example, the top of Figure 5.3 shows a selected frame from an annotated animation on lightning formation in which a sentence describing the movement of air is separated from a corresponding animation segment depicting the movement of air. As you can see, the text about movement of air is printed at the bottom of the screen, whereas the action takes place in areas away from the text.

On the other hand, an integration strategy means placing graphics and corresponding words as near to each other as possible. For example, the bottom of Figure 5.3 shows a selected frame from an annotated animation on lightning formation in which sentences describing steps

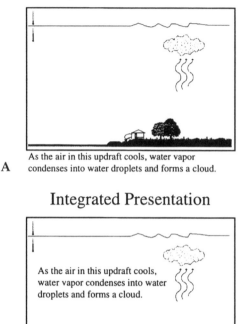

Figure 5.3 Example frames from **(A)** separated and **(B)** integrated computer-based multimedia presentation.

in lightning formation are integrated with corresponding animation segments depicting the same steps. As can be seen, the text about the movement of air is printed next to the corresponding animation action – that is, the wavy lines moving from left to right.

In both cases, the learner is presented with the same words and the same graphics, but corresponding animation segments and on-screen text sentences are far apart in the separated version and near one another in the integrated version. Which arrangement is most successful in fostering learning? In the next two sections, I explore the case for separating words and pictures and the case for integrating words and pictures, respectively.

The Case for Separating Words and Pictures

Common sense (and a long history of research on verbal learning) dictates that presenting the same material twice will result in students' learning more than presenting it once. This is what happens in the separated version of the lightning lesson: The learner first studies the words that describe steps in lightning formation and then studies the pictures that depict the same steps. By separating the words and pictures, we can expose learners to each step twice.

The case for separating words and pictures is based on an information-delivery theory of multimedia learning in which visual and verbal modes of presentation are posited to be separate routes for delivering information to the learner. When the same information is delivered at different times – as is the case for separated lessons – it has a greater effect because the learner has two chances to store it in memory. In contrast, when words and pictures describing the same information are delivered at the same time – as in the case of integrated lessons – it has less effect because the learner has only one chance to store it.

On the basis of the information-delivery theory, we can predict that separated presentations will result in more learning than will integrated presentations, as measured by tests of retention and, to some extent, by tests of transfer. In short, two separate exposures to the same material are better than one.

The Case for Integrating Words and Pictures

What's wrong with this straightforward, commonsense case for separating words and pictures in multimedia presentations? My major objection is that it is based on an incomplete view of how people learn – the idea that learning involves adding presented information to one's memory. In contrast, the cognitive theory of multimedia learning is based on the idea that learning is an active process in which the learner strives to make sense of the presented material. This sense-making effort is supported when corresponding words and pictures can be mentally integrated in the learner's working memory.

In the integrated version of the lesson, words and pictures are presented in a way that encourages learners to build mental connections between them. Learners do not have to search the screen or page to find a graphic that corresponds to a printed sentence; therefore, they can devote their cognitive resources to the processes of active learning, including building connections between words and pictures. According to the cognitive theory of multimedia learning, meaningful multimedia learning depends on building connections between mental representations of corresponding words and pictures. Thus, integrated presentations foster understanding that is reflected in performance on transfer tests, and to some extent on retention tests.

In separated versions of the lesson, words and pictures are presented in a way that discourages learners from building mental connections between them. Learners must search the screen or page to try to find a graphic that corresponds to a printed sentence; this process requires a cognitive effort that could have been used to support the processes of active learning. Thus, separated presentations are less likely to foster understanding than are integrated presentations.

On the basis of this analysis, the cognitive theory of multimedia learning predicts better retention and transfer from integrated presentations than from separated presentations. This pattern can be called a spatial contiguity effect because learning is improved when corresponding words and pictures are presented near each other – that is, when they are contiguous in space. In short, the case for integrated presentations is that they serve as aids for building cognitive connections between words and pictures.

Distinction between Multimedia Effect and Spatial Contiguity Effect

In the previous chapter, I presented evidence for a multimedia effect in which students understand a scientific explanation more deeply when it is presented using words and pictures rather than words alone. In each experimental test comparing single and multimedia presentations, the multimedia presentations were integrated – that is, printed words were always presented near their corresponding graphics. In this chapter, I extend this research by exploring one of the conditions under which multimedia presentations work; that is, I examine the role of the spatial arrangement of printed words and pictures on the page or screen. In particular, my goal is to determine whether there is a spatial contiguity effect in which students learn more when printed words and pictures are near rather than far from each other on the page or screen. Instead of asking whether multimedia works – a question addressed in the previous chapter on the multimedia effect – in this chapter and the following ones, I am interested in the conditions under which multimedia works.

RESEARCH ON SPATIAL CONTIGUITY

In a multimedia presentation consisting of printed text and graphics, should corresponding text and graphics be near or far from each other on the page or screen? My colleagues and I addressed this question in a series of five experimental tests (Mayer, 1989b, Experiment 1; Mayer,

Steinhoff, Bower, & Mars, 1995, Experiments 1, 2, and 3; Moreno & Mayer, 1999, Experiment 1). In each test, we compared the learning outcomes of learners who received separated multimedia presentations with those who received integrated multimedia presentations. In some studies, the separated and integrated presentations were in book-based environments (Mayer, 1989, Experiment 1; Mayer et al., 1995, Experiments 1, 2, and 3), such as shown respectively in Figures 5.1 and 5.2; in another study (Moreno & Mayer, 1999, Experiment 1), they were in computer-based environments, such as exemplified respectively in the top and bottom of Figure 5.3. In all cases, learning outcomes were assessed by asking students to write down the explanation they had learned (i.e., retention test) and to generate as many solutions as possible to a series of problem-solving transfer questions (i.e., transfer test). According to the information-delivery theory, students who learn from the separated presentation will perform better on retention and transfer tests than will students who learn from the integrated presentation, whereas the cognitive theory of multimedia learning makes the opposite prediction.

Spatial Contiguity Effect for Retention

Figure 5.4 shows the mean retention scores for students who received printed text and pictures near each other on the page or screen (integrated presentation group) and far from each other (separated presentation group). As you can see, for both tests, students in the integrated group remembered more of the explanation than did students in the

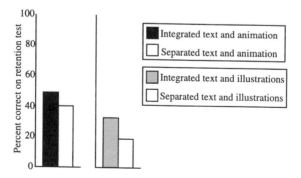

Figure 5.4 Spatial contiguity effect for retention: better retention when corresponding words and pictures are presented near (*dark bars*) rather than far from one another (*white bars*).

separated group. We refer to this pattern as a *spatial contiguity effect for retention* because placing corresponding words and pictures in spatial contiguity – that is, next to each other – resulted in better performance on retention tests. The spatial contiguity effect for retention is that students perform better on verbal retention when corresponding words and pictures are presented near rather than far from each other. Figure 5.5 shows the effect size and percentage gain for each test: The effect sizes are moderate to large with a median of .95 and the percentage gain is small to moderate, with a median of 42%. These results can be summarized by saying that on average, learners who received integrated presentations recalled about 1 standard deviation's worth more explanation material (or about 42% more explanation material) than did students who received separated presentations.

Overall, the results are inconsistent with the information-delivery theory and are consistent with the cognitive theory of multimedia learning. Importantly, the same pattern of results was obtained in a book-based environment (Mayer, 1989b, Experiment 2) as in a computer-based environment (Moreno & Mayer, 1999, Experiment 1). However, the major focus of our research is on transfer performance, which is reviewed in the next section.

Spatial Contiguity Effect for Transfer

Although the pattern of performance on the retention test is most consistent with the cognitive theory of multimedia learning, performance on the transfer test provides a better evaluation of how well students understood the explanation. Figure 5.6 shows the mean transfer scores for students who received printed text and pictures near each other on the page or screen (integrated presentation group) and far from each other (separated presentation group). In five of five tests, students in the integrated group generated more solutions to the problem-solving transfer questions than did students in the separated group. This pattern constitutes a *spatial contiguity effect for transfer* because placing corresponding words and pictures in spatial contiguity – that is, next to each other – resulted in

Figure 5.5 Spatial Contiguity Effect for Retention: Summary of Results

Source	Content	Effect size	Percent gain
Moreno and Mayer, 1999, Exp. 1	Lightning	.47	17
Mayer, 1989, Exp. 2	Brakes	1.44	68
Median		**.95**	**42**

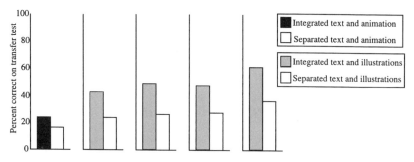

Figure 5.6 Spatial contiguity effect for transfer: better transfer when corresponding words and pictures are presented near (*dark bars*) rather than far from one another (*white bars*).

better performance on transfer tests. The spatial contiguity effect for transfer is that students perform better on transfer when corresponding words and pictures are presented near rather than far from each other. Figure 5.7 shows the effect size and percentage gain for each test: The effect sizes are moderate to large, with a median of 1.12, and the percentage gain is moderate, with a median of 68%. In sum, learners who received integrated presentations generated an average of about 1 standard deviation's worth more solutions (or about 68% more solutions) on problem-solving transfer tests than did students who received separated presentations.

As with the retention test results, the transfer test results are inconsistent with the information-delivery theory and are consistent with the cognitive theory of multimedia learning. Also consistent with the retention test results, the same pattern of transfer results was obtained in a book-based environment (Mayer, 1989b, Experiment 2; Mayer et al., 1995, Experiments 1, 2, and 3) as in a computer-based environment (Moreno & Mayer, 1999, Experiment 1). The effect appears to be stronger in the book-based environment, but this may be attributable to methodological differences. In particular, in the separated presenta-

Figure 5.7 Spatial Contiguity Effect for Transfer: Summary of Results

Source	Content	Effect size	Percent gain
Moreno and Mayer, 1999, Exp. 1	Lightning	.48	43
Mayer et al., 1995, Exp. 1	Lightning	1.09	78
Mayer et al., 1995, Exp. 2	Lightning	1.35	89
Mayer et al., 1995, Exp. 3	Lightning	1.12	68
Mayer, 1989, Exp. 2	Brakes	1.71	65
Median		**1.12**	**68**

tion, the words and pictures are farther apart in the book-based materials (i.e., on separate pages) than in the computer-based material (i.e., a few inches apart on the computer screen). Further research may be needed to create equivalent kinds of separated presentations for books and computers.

Related Research on Spatial Contiguity

Research on illustrations in textbooks shows that the majority of textbook illustrations fail to serve a useful educational purpose (Britton, Woodward, & Binkley, 1993; Levin & Mayer, 1993; Mayer, 1993b; Mayer, Sims, & Tajika, 1995). However, even when potentially useful illustrations are used, the way they are placed on the page (or on the computer screen) can greatly affect their pedagogic impact. In addition to the five demonstrations of spatial contiguity effects that I described above (based on Mayer, 1989b; Mayer et al., 1995; and Moreno & Mayer, 1999), similar patterns have been noted by other researchers (Chandler & Sweller, 1991; Paas & Van Merrienboer, 1994; Sweller & Chandler, 1994; Sweller, Chandler, Tierney, & Cooper, 1990).

The pattern of results that we call a spatial contiguity effect has been described by other researchers under the more general name of *split-attention effect* (Chandler & Sweller, 1992; Sweller et al., 1990; Tarmizi & Sweller, 1988). Sweller and his colleagues define the split-attention effect as any impairment in learning that occurs when a learner must mentally integrate disparate sources of information, and they have demonstrated it in the context of learning from worked-out examples (Chandler & Sweller, 1992; Cooper & Sweller, 1987; Sweller & Cooper, 1985; Ward & Sweller, 1990), learning computer programming (Chandler & Sweller, 1992; Sweller & Chandler, 1994; Sweller et al., 1990), and learning to perform a manual task (Bobis, Sweller, & Cooper, 1993). For example, learning computer programming was more difficult when the learner had to use both a manual and a computer than when all the needed material was contained in the manual (Chandler & Sweller, 1992; Sweller & Chandler, 1994).

Hegarty, Carpenter, and Just (1996) offer evidence, based on recording students' eye movements, showing that students can use text to guide their processing of accompanying illustrations. For example, when viewing a screen showing a diagram of a pulley system and text describing it (as in our integrated presentations), students read one or two sentences of text, then inspected the portion of the diagram that was described, then read one or two more sentences, then inspected a new portion of the diagram that was described, and so on. Consistent with the cognitive theory of multimedia learning, the process of integrating words and pictures appears to proceed in small chunks.

IMPLICATIONS

Implications for Multimedia Learning

What makes an effective multimedia message? Research on the *spatial contiguity effect* pinpoints one of the conditions under which multimedia instruction helps people understand a scientific explanation – namely, when the corresponding printed words and illustrations (or animations) are near each other on the page or screen. The spatial contiguity effect can be summarized as follows: Presenting corresponding words and pictures near each other on the page or screen results in better learning than presenting them far from each other.

These results conflict with the predictions of the information-delivery theory, which assumes that two separate presentations of the same material are better than one. For example, when a page containing a text passage on lightning formation is followed by a page containing illustrations depicting lightning formation, the learner is essentially exposed to the same explanation two times. The premise of the information-delivery theory is that verbal and visual presentations are simply routes for delivering information to a learner. According to this view, separated multimedia presentations allow for delivering information via one route and then delivering the same information via another route.

Given the failure to support the predictions based on information-delivery theory, is it possible to revive the information-delivery theory? Perhaps the interpretation of the theory was too strong, so let's consider a somewhat milder interpretation of the information-delivery theory. It is important to note that the same materials – the same words and pictures – were presented in the integrated and separated presentations, so the same information was delivered under both treatments. Therefore, we can conclude that students in the integrated and separated groups should perform at equivalent levels on tests of retention and transfer. Even if we take this somewhat more lenient approach to the information-delivery theory, the results conflict with our predictions because students consistently performed better on retention and transfer when they received the integrated rather than the separated presentation.

Why did the information-delivery theory – in its strong or mild form – fail to generate supportable predictions? One problem is that it is based on an incomplete view of how people learn scientific explanations. According to the information-delivery view, presented material is simply information that the learners add to their memories. This account may be accurate when the learning task is a collection of arbitrary fragments, such as a list of unrelated nonsense syllables, but it does not provide a complete explanation of how people learn conceptually deeper material.

In contrast, the results presented in this chapter are consistent with the cognitive theory of multimedia learning. According to this view, learners engage in active cognitive processing in an attempt to make sense out of the presented material. When they read an explanation of how lightning works and see illustrations depicting how lightning works, they are not simply trying to add the information to memory for storage. They are also trying to understand the material by actively selecting relevant words and images, organizing them into coherent verbal and visual mental models, and integrating the models. We refer to this as the active-learning assumption of the cognitive theory of multimedia learning.

When corresponding words and pictures are placed near rather than far from each other on the page or screen, the learner is better able to carry out this integration process. The rationale follows from the dual-channel assumption (i.e., the idea that humans possess separate verbal and visual information processing channels), the limited-capacity assumption (i.e., the idea that each channel has a limited amount of cognitive capacity), and the active-processing assumption (i.e., the idea that meaningful learning depends on processes such as selecting, organizing, and integrating). Consider how the limited cognitive capacity is used for separated and integrated presentations: For separated presentations, cognitive capacity is used to visually search for words or graphics on the page or screen, so less cognitive processing can be devoted to the integration process; for integrated presentations, the learner is guided in how to integrate corresponding words and pictures, so the integration process is more likely to occur.

In sum, our results are consistent with the three major assumptions underlying the cognitive theory of multimedia learning – dual channels, limited capacity, and active processing. In contrast, the information-delivery view appears to be inadequate in our quest for design principles for multimedia messages.

Implications for Multimedia Design

Our results show that meaningful learning from multimedia presentations depends not just on presenting the necessary information – both the separated and integrated messages presented the same material – but rather on presenting the necessary information along with guidance to the learner for how to mentally process it. The fact that integrated presentation resulted in deeper learning than did separated presentation encourages us to consider ways to arrange words and pictures that are most compatible with ways that people learn.

The research in this chapter allows us to offer an important principle for the design of multimedia explanations: Present words and pictures near rather than far from each other. In book-based contexts, this means that illustrations should be placed next to the sentences that describe them, or better, the most relevant phrases may be placed within the illustrations themselves. In computer-based contexts, this means that on-screen text should be presented next to the graphics that they describe.

This spatial contiguity principle provides a first step in pinpointing the conditions that lead to deeper learning from multimedia presentations. It focuses mainly on the contiguous spatial arrangement of printed text and illustrations on a textbook page (or on a computer screen). In the next chapter, I explore an analogous principle concerning the contiguous temporal arrangement of spoken text and animation in a computer-based context. Thus, whereas chapter 5 focuses on contiguous arrangement of words and pictures in space, chapter 6 focuses on their contiguous arrangement in time.

SUGGESTED READINGS

*Mayer, R. E. (1989). Systematic thinking fostered by illustrations in scientific text. *Journal of Educational Psychology, 81,* 240–246.

*Mayer, R. E., Steinhoff, K., Bower, G. & Mars, R. (1995). A generative theory of textbook design: Using annotated illustrations to foster meaningful learning of science text. *Educational Technology Research and Development, 43,* 31–43.

*Moreno, R., & Mayer, R. E. (1999). Cognitive principles of multimedia learning: The role of modality and contiguity. *Journal of Educational Psychology, 91,* 358–368.

---

*Asterisk indicates that part of this chapter is based on this publication.

6

Temporal Contiguity Principle

Temporal Contiguity Principle: Students learn better when corresponding words and pictures are presented simultaneously rather than successively.

Theoretical Rationale: When corresponding portions of narration and animation are presented at the same time, the learner is more likely to be able to hold mental representations of both in working memory at the same time, and thus the learner is more likely to be able to build mental connections between verbal and visual representations. When corresponding portions of narration and animation are separated in time, the learner is less likely to be able to hold mental representations of both in working memory at the same time and thus less likely to be able to build mental connections between verbal and visual representations. If the time between hearing a sentence and seeing the corresponding portion of animation is short, then the learner may still be able to build connections between words and pictures. However, if the learner hears a long passage and views an entire animation at separate times, then the learner is less likely to be build connections between words and pictures.

Empirical Rationale: In three of five tests, learners performed better on retention tests when corresponding portions of animation and narration were presented simultaneously rather than successively. In eight of eight tests, learners performed better on transfer tests when corresponding portions of animation and narration were presented simultaneously rather than successively. In addition, when the successive presentation was based on very short segments – such as a sentence describing one action and a few seconds of animation depicting one action – there was no strong temporal contiguity effect for retention (in three of three tests) or transfer (in three of three tests).

■ ■ Chapter Outline

INTRODUCTION
Time as an Economic Resource

INTRODUCTION

Time as an Economic Resource

In the previous chapter, I made the argument that page space (or screen space) is a scarce resource. In deciding how to use space, such as where to put words and where to put pictures, instructional designers are making decisions about how to allocate scarce resources among alternative uses. This kind of decision corresponds to the classic definition of an economic decision.

The same argument applies to the allocation of time in a computer-based multimedia presentation. Time is a scarce resource, so decisions must be made about where to place words and where to place pictures within the temporal sequence. Again, in deciding how to allocate the scarce resource of time among alternative uses, instructional designers are faced with an economic decision.

Suppose you have been asked to create a short multimedia presentation on the formation of lightning to be included as an entry in a multimedia encyclopedia. You can use words, such as narration or on-screen text, and you can use pictures, such as animation and illustrations. Let's assume that you have developed a narration describing the major steps in lightning formation – consisting of 300 words broken down into 16 segments, such as shown in Figure 6.1. Let's also assume that you have developed a series of 16 animation segments depicting these same steps in lightning formation and lasting a total of 140 seconds. Some selected frames are shown in Figure 2.1. If the 16 narration segments and 16 animation segments are your

1. Cool, moist air moves over a warmer surface and becomes heated.
2. Warmed moist air near the earth's surface rises rapidly.
3. As the air in this updraft cools, water vapor condenses into water droplets and forms a cloud.
4. The cloud's top extends above the freezing level, so the upper portion of the cloud is composed of tiny ice crystals.
5. Within the cloud, the rising and falling air currents cause electrical charges to build.
6. The charge results from the collision of the cloud's rising water droplets against heavier, falling pieces of ice.
7. The negatively charged particles fall to the bottom of the cloud, and most of the positively charged particles rise to the top.
8. Eventually, the water droplets and ice crystals become too large to be suspended by the updrafts.
9. As raindrops and ice crystals fall through the cloud, they drag some of the air in the cloud downward, producing downdrafts.
10. When downdrafts strike the ground, they spread out in all directions, producing the gusts of cool wind people feel just before the start of the rain.
11. A stepped leader of negative charges moves downward in a series of steps. It nears the ground.
12. A positively charged leader travels up from such objects as trees and buildings.
13. The two leaders generally meet about 165 feet above the ground.
14. Negatively charged particles then rush from the cloud to the ground along the path created by the leaders. It is not very bright.
15. As the leader stroke nears the ground, it induces an opposite charge, so positively charged particles from the ground rush upward along the same path.
16. This upward motion of the current is the return stroke. It produces the bright light that people notice as a flash of lightning.

Figure 6.1 Sixteen segments of narration script for lightning lesson.

building blocks, how would you go about using them to create a short multimedia presentation?

A straightforward approach is to present the entire narration and then the entire animation (or vice versa). In this way, the learner can first pay attention to the verbal description of lightning formation and then pay attention to a visual depiction of lightning formation (or vice versa). We refer to this as successive presentation because all the words are presented before all the pictures (or vice versa). In this case, corresponding words and pictures are not contiguous in time, so there is a lack of what we call temporal contiguity.

An alternative approach is to present the narration and animation at the same time in close coordination so that when the narration describes a particular action in words, the animation depicts the same action visually at the same time. In this way, the learner sees and hears about the same step at the same time. We refer to this as simultaneous presentation because corresponding segments of words and pictures are presented at the same time. In this case, the corresponding words and pictures are contiguous in time, creating what we call temporal contiguity.

Which is better for your multimedia encyclopedia entry – successive or simultaneous presentation? In many cases, decisions about how to use time in multimedia presentations are based on the best intuitions of the designers, on design principles that may not have a solid research base, or simply on the need to present a certain amount of information in an entertaining way. In this chapter, I take a more scientific approach by exploring some research we have conducted over the years at the University of California, Santa Barbara. The purpose of the research is to examine the cognitive consequences of learning from successive and simultaneous presentations and thereby contribute both to a theory of multimedia learning and to a research-based set of multimedia design principles.

As with research on spatial contiguity, our goal in examining temporal contiguity is to determine the conditions under which multimedia presentations are most likely to promote meaningful learning. In successive and simultaneous presentations, the same material is presented – the same animation and the same narration. Both are multimedia presentations because both contain words and pictures. The crucial difference between successive and simultaneous presentations is the way in which time is used for presenting the narration and animation.

In the next sections, I examine the case for successive multimedia presentations on the basis of an information-delivery theory of multimedia learning and the case for simultaneous presentations on the basis of a cognitive theory of multimedia learning.

The Case for Separating Words and Pictures

Common sense tells us that people will learn more from two exposures to the same material than from one exposure. The successive-presentation format allows for two separate exposures – first, learners can devote their full attention to a verbal description of how lightning storms develop, and next, they can devote their full attention to a visual depiction of the same events (or they can attend to the visual presentation followed by the verbal presentation). The simultaneous-presentation format allows for only one exposure because each of the sixteen major events is presented only once – with the verbal description and visual depiction happening at the same time. In terms of time, learners who receive the successive presentation get to spend twice as much time studying the material as compared to learners who receive the simultaneous presentation.

This commonsense analysis is based on the information-delivery view of multimedia learning in which learning involves placing presented information into one's memory for long-term storage. When you receive two deliveries – first a delivery via the word route and then a delivery via the picture route, or vice versa – you have a greater chance of placing more information in memory. When you receive one delivery – which comes via two separate routes – you have fewer opportunities to add information into your memory.

According to the information-delivery theory, students who receive successive presentations should learn more than students who receive simultaneous presentations. Thus, the theory predicts that students given successive presentations should outperform students given simultaneous presentations on tests of retention and, to some extent, on tests of transfer.

The Case for Integrating Words and Pictures

The successive-presentation format seems to be an obvious choice for maximizing the impact of animation and narration. What's wrong with the case for temporally separating words and pictures? As in chapter 5, my main objection to separating words and pictures is that it is based on an incomplete conception of how people learn. According to the cognitive theory of multimedia learning, humans are not information storage machines who receive deliveries of information and store the deliveries in memory. Instead, humans are sense makers who engage in active cognitive processes such as selecting relevant words and pictures, organizing the selected material into verbal and visual mental models, and integrating the verbal and visual models.

On the basis of a cognitive theory of multimedia learning, I propose that students are more likely to be able to understand multimedia presentations when corresponding words and pictures are available in working memory at the same time. Simultaneous presentation increases the chances that a learner will be able to hold corresponding visual and verbal representations of the same event in working memory at the same time. This increases the chances that the learner will be able to mentally integrate the verbal and visual representations – a major cognitive process in meaningful learning.

Simultaneous presentations are designed to mesh with the human information processing system – including the availability of separate visual and verbal channels as well as the extreme limits on the capacity of each channel. Narration can be processed in the verbal channel while the corresponding animation segment is processed in the visual channel. That is, as students see cool (blue-colored) air moving over a warmer surface and become heated (red-colored) through their visual channel, they can also hear "Cool, moist air moves over a warmer surface and becomes heated" through their verbal channel. Although cognitive capacity is limited, there is enough cognitive capacity to hold each of these representations and to make connections between them.

In contrast, on the basis of the cognitive theory of multimedia learning, I propose that students are less likely to be able to understand multimedia presentations when corresponding words and pictures are greatly separated in time. In successive presentations, learners process the entire narration before seeing the entire animation (or vice versa). Given the severe limits on working memory, only a small part of the narration remains in verbal working memory when the animation begins (or only a small portion of the animation remains in visual working memory when the narration begins). Thus, the student may have difficulty in building connections between words and pictures.

Successive presentations seem to conflict with the way that humans are designed to process information. Instead of taking advantage of our ability to simultaneously process material within our visual and verbal channels, successive presentations first present material to be processed in one channel and then present material to be processed in the other one. Instead of being sensitive to human limitations in working memory capacity, successive presentations require that a learner be able to hold the entire narration in working memory until the narration is presented (or vice versa) – an impossible feat, according to the cognitive theory of multimedia learning.

According to the cognitive theory of multimedia learning, the temporal arrangement of narration and animation in successive presentations fails to mesh with the way people's minds work, whereas the temporal arrangement of narration and animation in simultaneous presentations takes advantage of the way people's minds work. Even though successive and simultaneous presentations contain identical material – the same narration and the same animation – the cognitive theory of multimedia learning allows me to make quite different predictions: Students who receive simultaneous presentations are better able to understand the explanation than are students who receive successive presentations. This difference should be reflected in transfer test performance with simultaneous treatments leading to better transfer than do successive presentations. The predictions concerning verbal retention are less clear because two competing events are at work: (1) students in the simultaneous condition are more likely to make sense of the presented material and therefore are predicted to perform better on retention than are students in the successive condition, but (2) students in the successive condition are more likely to focus on the wording of the verbal presentation and therefore may be more likely to perform well on a test of verbal retention. Overall, I give more weight to the value of meaningful processing and therefore predict that students in the simultaneous group will outperform students in the successive group on tests of verbal retention.

Distinction between Spatial Contiguity and Temporal Contiguity

As you can see, the cases for separating or integrating words and pictures in time (as discussed in this chapter) are similar to cases for separating or integrating them in space (as discussed in chapter 5). Spatial contiguity and temporal contiguity are two related forms of contiguity in the design of multimedia presentations. Spatial contiguity deals with placing corresponding words and pictures close to each other on the page, whereas temporal continuity deals with presenting corresponding words and pictures close to each other in time. Both are based on the same underlying cognitive mechanisms – namely, that students are better able to build connections between words and pictures when they can mentally process them at the same time.

In spite of their similarities, spatial and temporal contiguity are not identical, so I have opted to discuss them in separate chapters and under separate names. Spatial contiguity is important for the layout of a page in textbook or a frame on a computer screen. Spatial contiguity involves material that is processed, at least initially, by the eyes – printed text, and graphics (such as illustrations or animations). In contrast, temporal contiguity is important for the timing of computer-based presentations. Temporal contiguity involves material that is processed by the eyes – for example, animation – and material that is processed by the ears – for example, narration. In this situation, the temporal processing of the material is controlled by the instructional designer – that is, the instructional designer can choose to present first only words and next only graphics, or vice versa.

RESEARCH ON TEMPORAL CONTIGUITY

Do students learn more deeply when corresponding narration and animation are present simultaneously than when they are presented successively, as proposed by the cognitive theory of multimedia learning? Or do students acquire more information from a multimedia presentation when animation and narration are presented successively than when they are presented simultaneously, as proposed by the information-delivery theory of multimedia learning?

To answer these questions, I review the results of eight experimental comparisons of students who learned from successive presentations versus students who learned from simultaneous presentations (Mayer & Anderson, 1991, Experiments 1 and Experiments 2a; Mayer & Anderson, 1992, Experiments 1 and Experiments 2; Mayer, Moreno, Boire, & Vagge, 1999, Experiments 1 and Experiments 2; Mayer & Sims, 1994, Experiments 1 and Experiments 2). In each test, we compared the retention and/or transfer performance of students who received successive presentations with the corresponding performance of those who received simultaneous presentations, including explanations of lightning formation (Mayer et al., 1999; Experiment 1), how the human respiratory system works (Mayer & Sims, 1994, Experiment 2), how car brakes work (Mayer & Anderson, 1992, Experiment 2; Mayer et al., 1999, Experiment 1; Mayer & Sims, 1994, Experiment 2), and how pumps work (Mayer & Anderson, 1991, Experiments 1 and 2a; Mayer & Anderson, 1992, Experiment 1). All experiments involved animation and narration presented in a computer-based environment, and all learners took the same retention and transfer tests as described in previous chapters. According to the information-delivery theory, the successive presentation should result in better learning than should the simultaneous presentation, whereas the cognitive theory of multimedia learning yields the opposite prediction.

Temporal Contiguity Effect for Retention

Figure 6.2 shows the mean retention scores for simultaneous and successive presentation groups in five separate experimental studies. In three of the five comparisons, the simultaneous group recalled more of the steps in the explanation than did the successive group. Thus, we obtained mixed evidence for what could be called a *temporal contiguity effect for retention*, namely, a pattern in which students learn better when corresponding segments of animation and narration are presented contiguously in time – that is, as near to each other as possible in time – than when they are separated by longer periods of time. In short, we found only mixed evidence for a temporal contiguity effect for retention because in only three of the five comparisons did students recall more of the relevant verbal material when it was presented concurrently with corresponding visual material

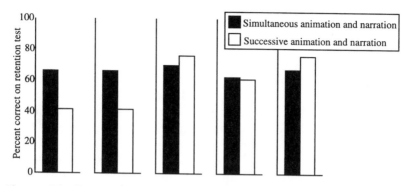

Figure 6.2   Temporal contiguity effect for retention: better retention when corresponding words and pictures are presented simultaneously (*dark bars*) rather than successively (*white bars*).

rather than when verbal and visual materials were presented successively. Figure 6.3 shows that the effect sizes were mixed, running from −.43 to +1.53, with a median of .03. Similarly, the percent gains were mixed, running from −12% to +62%, with a median of 0. On the basis of median scores, I conclude that there was not a strong temporal contiguity effect for retention.

Why did we fail to find a temporal contiguity effect for retention? In the simultaneous treatment, students were able to build a deeper understanding of the material, which should help them remember more of the important material. However, in the successive treatment, students were able to listen to the narration without any other distractions, which should help them in tests that are sensitive to verbatim verbal retention. Perhaps these two opposing forces canceled each other out, resulting in no temporal contiguity effect. More research is needed to determine the conditions under which simultaneous presentation fosters better retention than successive presentation.

Figure 6.3   Temporal Contiguity Effect for Retention: Summary of Results

Source	Content	Effect size	Percent gain
Mayer et al., 1999, Exp. 1	Lightning	1.05	62
Mayer et al., 1999, Exp. 2	Brakes	1.53	58
Mayer and Anderson, 1992, Exp. 1	Pumps	−.35	−.08
Mayer and Anderson, 1992, Exp. 2	Brakes	.03	.00
Mayer and Anderson, 1991, Exp. 2a	Pumps	−.43	−.12
Median		.03	0

Temporal Contiguity Effect for Transfer

The main focus of our research is on problem-solving transfer because transfer tests are intended to measure the learner's understanding of the presented material. Figure 6.4 shows the mean transfer scores for the simultaneous and successive groups across eight different experimental comparisons. As you can see, in eight of eight tests, students who received corresponding segments of animation and narration simultaneously performed much better on generating solutions to problems than did students who received the same segments successively. We refer to this pattern as a *temporal contiguity effect for transfer* because students learned more deeply when corresponding segments of animation and narration were contiguous in time (i.e., they occurred as close together as possible in time) than when they were separated in time.

Figure 6.5 shows that the effect sizes were large and consistent across the eight comparisons, with a median of 1.30. This means that students

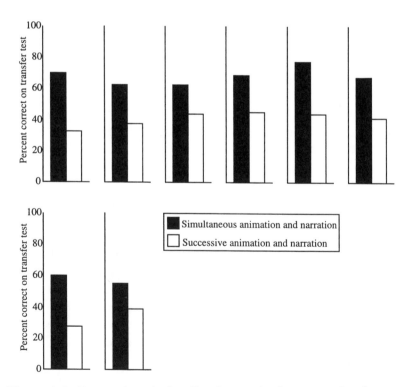

Figure 6.4   Temporal contiguity effect for transfer: better transfer when corresponding words and pictures are presented simultaneously (*dark bars*) rather than successively (*white bars*).

Figure 6.5 Temporal Contiguity Effect for Transfer: Summary of Results

Source	Content	Effect size	Percent gain
Mayer et al., 1999 Exp. 1	Lightning	1.96	115
Mayer et al., 1999, Exp. 2	Brakes	1.27	66
Mayer and Sims, 1994, Exp. 1	Brakes	.83	43
Mayer and Sims, 1994, Exp. 2	Lungs	1.60	57
Mayer and Anderson 1992, Exp. 1	Pumps	1.61	70
Mayer and Anderson, 1992, Exp. 2	Brakes	1.33	64
Mayer and Anderson, 1991, Exp. 1	Pumps	1.00	45
Mayer and Anderson, 1991, Exp. 2a	Pumps	1.05	48
Median		**1.30**	**60**

who learned from the simultaneous presentation generated an average of 1.30 standard deviation's worth more solutions on the problem-solving transfer test than did students who received the successive presentation. Similarly, Figure 6.5 shows that the percent gain of the simultaneous group over the successive group is large and consistent across the eight comparisons, with a median of 60%. This means that on average, the simultaneous groups produced 60% more solutions on the problem-solving transfer test than did the successive group.

Overall, the temporal contiguity effect is evidence in support of the cognitive theory of multimedia learning and against the information-delivery theory.

Extensions of the Temporal Contiguity Effect for Retention and Transfer

My colleagues and I carried out three related comparisons (Mayer et al., 1999, Experiments 1 and 2; Moreno & Mayer, 1999, Experiment 2), in which we compared the test performance of students who learned from a successive small-segments presentation and a simultaneous presentation. In the successive small-segments presentations, some students listened to a short portion of the narration describing one major step and then viewed a short animation segment depicting the same step, and so on for each of sixteen short segments (and other students viewed an animation segment followed by a corresponding narration segment and so on for each of sixteen short segments).

The simultaneous presentation treatment is the same as in the previously described experiments. The successive small-segments presentation is different from the successive presentation described for the previous experiments; the successive small-segments presentation involves many alternations between a short narration followed (or

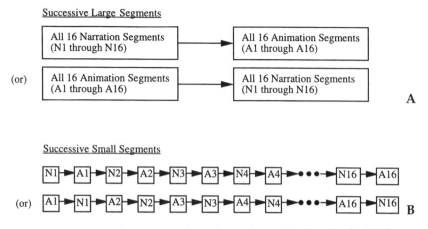

Figure 6.6 Successive presentation of narration and animation for **(A)** large segment (Top Frame) and **(B)** small segments (Bottom Frame) Note: the designations N1–N16 refer to the sixteen narration segments and A1–A16 refer to the 16 animation segments.

preceded) by a short animation, whereas the successive presentation involves the entire narration followed (or preceded) by the entire animation. In essence, the successive presentation in the previous studies involved successive large segments, whereas the successive presentation used in the follow-up studies included successive small segments. Figure 6.6 summarizes the successive large-segments presentation used in the previous studies (top panel) and the successive small-segments presentation used in these follow-up studies (bottom panel).

We created the successive small-segments presentation to provide an additional way of testing the information-delivery and cognitive theories of multimedia learning. According to the information-delivery theory, as in the previous studies, the successive small-segments presentation should result in better test performance than should the simultaneous presentation. In the successive small-segments version, students receive two exposures to the same material – one in verbal form followed (or preceded) by one in visual form. In addition, students in the successive small-segments group have twice as much time to study the material as compared with the students who receive the simultaneous presentation.

In contrast, consider what happens in the learner's information processing according to the cognitive theory of multimedia learning. In the successive small-segments group, students are able to hold a verbal description of a step in the explanation and a visual depiction of the same

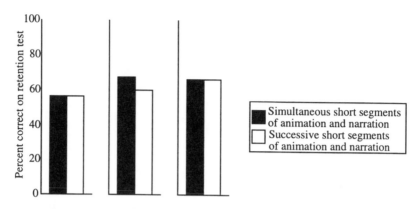

Figure 6.7 No small-segment temporal contiguity effect for retention: no difference in retention when corresponding short segments of words and pictures are presented simultaneously (*dark bars*) rather than successively (*white bars*).

step at the same time in their working memory, thus allowing students to mentally integrate corresponding visual and verbal material. The capacity of working memory is not exceeded, because the segments are short, thus enabling students to engage in meaningful learning. This situation contrasts with the successive large-segment presentations used in the previous experiments, where the entire narration was presented before (or after) the entire animation. In that case, there was less chance that corresponding verbal and visual representations would be in working memory at the same time. In short, the successive small-segments presentations enable the same kind of active cognitive processing as simultaneous presentations, so the cognitive theory of multimedia learning predicts no difference between the groups.

Figure 6.7 summarizes the retention scores of the simultaneous and successive small-segments presentation groups for each of three experimental tests. As you can see, there is not a strong temporal contiguity effect for retention; that is, presenting animation and narration simultaneously resulted in retention performance essentially equivalent to that for presenting animation and narration successively in small segments. Figure 6.8 shows that the effect sizes and percent gains were very small, with a median effect size of .03 and a median percent gain of 1%. On average, the simultaneous group remembered .03 standard deviation's worth more material than did the successive small-segments group; put another way, the simultaneous group remembered 1% more than did the successive small-segments groups. On the basis of statistical tests, we concluded that the difference is so small as to be negligible. This confirms the prediction of no large differences between the groups.

Figure 6.8   No Small-Segment Temporal Contiguity Effect for Retention: Summary of Results

Source	Content	Effect size	Percent gain
Moreno and Mayer, in press, Exp. 2	Lightning	.00	0
Mayer et al., 1999, Exp. 1	Lightning	.42	8
Mayer et al., 1999, Exp. 2	Brakes	.03	1
Median		**.03**	**1**

Figure 6.9 summarizes the transfer scores of the simultaneous and successive small-segments presentation groups for each of three experimental tests. As with the retention scores, there is not a strong temporal contiguity effect for transfer: Presenting animation and narration simultaneously resulted in transfer performance essentially equivalent to that of presenting animation and narration successively in small segments. Figure 6.10 shows that the effect sizes and percent gains were very small, with a median effect size of .12 and a median percent gain of 5%. On average, the simultaneous group generated .12 standard deviation's worth more solutions on the problem-solving transfer test than did the successive small-segments group; put another way, the simultaneous group produced 5% more solutions than did the successive small-segments groups. I judge the difference to be negligible, thus confirming the prediction of no large differences between the groups. These results are consistent with the cognitive theory of multimedia learning and inconsistent with the information-delivery theory.

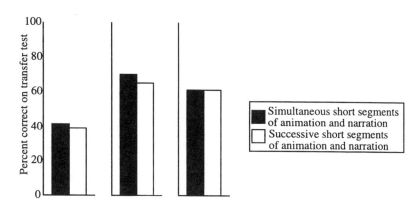

Figure 6.9   No small-segment temporal contiguity effect for transfer: no difference in transfer when corresponding short segments of words and pictures are presented simultaneously (*dark bars*) rather than successively (*white bars*).

Figure 6.10 No Small-Segment Temporal Contiguity Effect for Transfer: Summary of Results

Source	Content	Effect size	Percent gain
Moreno and Mayer, 1999 Exp. 2	Lightning	.12	5
Mayer et al., 1999, Exp. 1	Lightning	.24	8
Mayer et al., 1999, Exp. 2	Brakes	.05	1
Median		**.12**	**5**

Related Research on Temporal Contiguity

Research on temporal contiguity has its roots in classic studies by Baggett and her colleagues (Baggett, 1984; 1989; Baggett & Ehrenfeucht, 1983) in which students viewed films with voice overlay. The film showed how to use an assembly kit called Fischer Technik 50, which is similar to Lego sets, and the narration described the kit in words. For some students, the corresponding sounds and images were presented simultaneously (as in our simultaneous group); for others, the sound track preceded the corresponding visual material by 7, 14, or 21 seconds or the sound track followed the visual material by 7, 14, or 21 seconds (similar to our successive group). After the multimedia presentation, students were tested on their memory of the names of the pieces in the assembly kit. In particular, for each test item, they were shown a piece and asked to write down its name. Students who received the simultaneous presentation performed better on the test than did students in the other groups, with those who received the visual and verbal materials separated by 14 or 21 seconds performing particularly poorly. This pattern reflects a temporal contiguity effect. The research reported in this chapter extends Baggett's classic work by using tests that are intended to measure understanding rather than solely retention, by using multimedia materials that provide a cause-and-effect explanation rather than a nonconceptual description, and by comparing simultaneous presentations to successive ones rather than to ones in which the sound and images are misaligned.

Other researchers have used the term *split-attention effect* to refer to any situation in which the learner must process incoming information from diverse sources, and in particular, they have referred to the temporal contiguity effect as a "temporal example of split attention" (Mousavi, Low, & Sweller, 1995, p. 320). I prefer to separate the various forms of split attention because they translate more directly into clear design principles; therefore, in this book I devote separate chapters to spatial contiguity effects, temporal contiguity effects, and modality effects, all of which could be considered forms of split attention.

IMPLICATIONS

Implications for Multimedia Learning

The research results reported in this chapter are largely inconsistent with the information-delivery theory of multimedia learning and its commonsense notion that two deliveries of the same information must be better than one. Clearly, our results show that something is wrong with the seemingly obvious idea that learning occurs when students add presented information to their memory. In particular, the research on temporal contiguity fails to support the prediction that the successive group will outperform the simultaneous group.

In contrast, research on temporal contiguity provides consistent support for the cognitive theory of multimedia learning. Overall, when animation and narration are separated in time by more than a few seconds, students perform more poorly on problem-solving transfer than when animation and narration are presented simultaneously (or very near each other in time). We refer to this finding as a *temporal contiguity effect*: Separating corresponding words and pictures in time detracts from multimedia learning. Interestingly, the successive and simultaneous groups did not show a consistent difference on retention, but they differed strongly and consistently on transfer, which is intended to measure understanding.

Why does simultaneous presentation aid students in their quest for making sense of a multimedia explanation? According to the cognitive theory of multimedia learning, simultaneous presentations mesh well with the way that humans are designed to process incoming material – that is, simultaneous presentations are more consistent with the way the human mind works. In particular, simultaneous presentations take advantage of (1) the dual-channel capabilities of humans by providing narration to the ears and animation to the eyes, (2) the limited capacity of each channel by not requiring that learners hold a lot of material in either channel, and (3) the need for active cognitive processing by encouraging learners to make connections between corresponding visual and verbal representations.

Implications for Multimedia Design

The temporal contiguity effect yields an important design principle: Present words and pictures near rather than far from each other in time. As you can see, this principle complements the spatial contiguity principle, which calls for presenting words and pictures near rather than far from each other on the page or screen. Together, these two contiguity principles form the basis of our premier recommendations for how to design understandable multimedia messages. If we want students to build cognitive connections between corresponding words and pictures, it is helpful to present them contiguously in time and space – that is, to present them at the same time or next to each other on the page or screen.

The temporal contiguity effect provides an important example of what is wrong with assuming that the instructional designer's job is to present information. Even though the simultaneous and successive presentations contain the same animation and narration, students do not appear to learn equally from them. Apparently, students also benefit from some guidance concerning how to process the incoming material. Simultaneous presentations prime the learner to build connections between corresponding visual and verbal material, whereas successive presentations make this active cognitive processing much more difficult. Thus, instructional design involves not just presenting information but also presenting it in a way that encourages learners to engage in appropriate cognitive processing.

SUGGESTED READINGS

*Mayer, R. E., & Anderson, R. B. (1991). Animations need narrations: An experimental test of a dual-coding hypothesis. *Journal of Educational Psychology, 83,* 484–490.

*Mayer, R. E., & Anderson, R. B. (1992). The instructive animation: Helping students build connections between words and pictures in multimedia learning. *Journal of Educational Psychology, 84,* 444–452.

*Mayer, R. E., Moreno, R., Boire, M., & Vagge, S. (1999). Maximizing constructivist learning from multimedia communications by minimizing cognitive load. *Journal of Educational Psychology, 91,* 638–643.

*Mayer, R. E., & Sims, V. K. (1994). For whom is a picture worth a thousand words? Extensions of a dual-coding theory of multimedia learning. *Journal of Educational Psychology, 84,* 389–401.

*Moreno, R., & Mayer, R. E. (1999). Cognitive principles of multimedia learning: The role of modality and contiguity. *Journal of Educational Psychology, 91,* 358–368.

---

* Asterisk indicates that part of this chapter is based on this publication.

7 | Coherence Principle

Coherence Principle: *Students learn better when extraneous material is excluded rather than included. The coherence principle can be broken into three complementary versions: (1) student learning is hurt when interesting but irrelevant words and pictures are added to a multimedia presentation; (2) student learning is hurt when interesting but irrelevant sounds and music are added to a multimedia presentation; and (3) student learning is improved when unneeded words are eliminated from a multimedia presentation. Each version of the coherence principle is addressed in turn in this chapter.*

Theoretical Rationale: *Extraneous material competes for cognitive resources in working memory and can divert attention from the important material, can disrupt the process of organizing the material, and can prime the learner to organize the material around an inappropriate theme.*

Empirical Rationale: *In eleven of eleven tests, learners who received concise multimedia presentations performed better on tests of retention than did learners who received multimedia messages that contained extraneous material. In eleven of eleven tests, learners who received concise multimedia presentations performed better on tests of transfer than did learners who received multimedia messages that contained extraneous material.*

▪▪ Chapter Outline

COHERENCE PRINCIPLE 1: Student Learning is Hurt When Interesting but Irrelevant Words and Pictures Are Added to a Multimedia Presentation
    Introduction
        How Can We Improve Multimedia Presentations?
        The Case for Adding Interesting Words and Pictures
        The Case Against Adding Interesting Words and Pictures

All of the materials we used in our research provide cause-and-effect explanations of how scientific systems work in which a change in one part of the system is logically related to a change in another part, and so on. *Coherence* refers to the structural relations among elements in a message, such as the cause-and-effect chain in our explanations. A potentially coherent message is one in which the elements are related to one another in a nonarbitrary way, such as a cause-and-effect chain. A *coherence effect* occurs when students better understand an explanation from a multimedia lesson containing less material than from a multimedia lesson containing more material. In this chapter, I examine three variations of the theme: (1) adding interesting but irrelevant text or illustrations hurts learning; (2) adding interesting but extraneous sounds or music hurts learning; and (3) removing nonessential words improves learning.

COHERENCE PRINCIPLE 1: STUDENT LEARNING IS HURT WHEN INTERESTING BUT IRRELEVANT WORDS AND PICTURES ARE ADDED TO A MULTIMEDIA PRESENTATION

Introduction

How Can We Improve Multimedia Presentations?

Figure 7.1 presents a short lesson on how lightning storms develop, including illustrations depicting the major steps pictorially and corresponding text describing the major steps in words. It is a multimedia presentation because the explanation is presented both in words and pictures. The lesson is consistent with many of the design principles

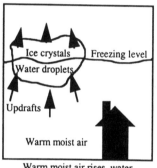

Warm moist air rises, water vapor condenses and forms a cloud.

When the surface of the earth is warm, moist air near the earth's surface becomes heated and rises rapidly, producing an updraft. As the air in these updrafts cools, water vapor condenses into water droplets and forms a cloud. The cloud's top extends above the freezing level. At this altitude, the air temperature is well below freezing, so the upper portion of the cloud is composed of tiny ice crystals.

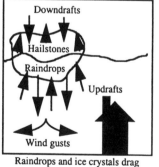

Raindrops and ice crystals drag air downward.

Eventually, the water droplets and ice crystals in the cloud become too large to be suspended by updrafts. As raindrops and ice crystals fall through the cloud, they drag some of the air from the cloud downward, producing downdrafts. The rising and falling air currents within the cloud may cause hailstones to form. When downdrafts strike the ground, they spread out in all directions, producing gusts of cool wind people feel just before the start of the rain.

(continues)

Figure 7.1 A portion of a multimedia lesson on lightning.

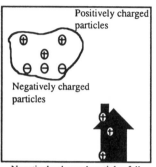

Negatively charged particles fall
to the bottom of the cloud.

Within the cloud, the moving air causes electrical charges to build, although scientists do not fully understand how it occurs. Most believe that the charge results from the collision of the cloud's light, rising water droplets and tiny pieces of ice against hail and other heavier, falling particles. The negatively charged particles fall to the bottom of the cloud, and most of the positively charged particles rise to the top.

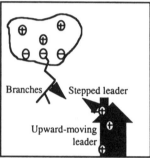

Two leaders meet, negatively
charged particles rush from the
cloud to the ground.

The first stroke of a cloud-to-ground lightning flash is started by a stepped leader. Many scientists believe that it is triggered by a spark between the areas of positive and negative charges within the cloud. A stepped leader moves downward in a series of steps, each of which is about 50-yards long, and lasts for about 1 millionth of a second. It pauses between steps for about 50 millionths of a second. As the stepped leader nears the ground, positively charged upward-moving leaders travel up from such objects as trees and buildings, to meet the negative charges. Usually, the upward moving leader from the tallest object is the first to meet the stepped leader and complete a path between the cloud and earth. The two leaders generally meet about 165-feet above the ground. Negatively charged particles then rush from the cloud to the ground along the path created by the leaders. It is not very bright and usually has many branches.

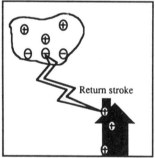

Positively charged particles from
the ground rush upward along the
same path.

As the stepped leader nears the ground, it induces an opposite charge, so positively charged particles from the ground rush upward along the same path. This upward motion of the current is the return stoke and it reaches the cloud in about 70 microseconds. The return stoke produces the bright light that people notice in a flash of lightning, but the current moves so quickly that its upward motion cannot be perceived. The lightning flash usually consists of an electrical potential of hundreds of millions of volts. The air along the lightning channel is heated briefly to a very high temperature. Such intense heating causes the air to expand explosively, producing a sound wave we call thunder.

Figure 7.1 Continued.

suggested in previous chapters because it combines words and pictures in an integrated way. What can you do to improve on this lesson, so that students will remember more of the important information and be able to use it to solve problems?

One seemingly reasonable suggestion is to spice up the lesson by adding some text and pictures intended to make the lesson more interesting. For example, we could add a short story about a high school football player who was struck by lightning during football practice, and show a picture of the hole it produced in his helmet and uniform. Also, we could add a description of what happens when lightning strikes a golfer and show a picture of a lightning-scorched putting green. Figure 7.2 shows some interesting material that can be added to another part of the lesson, including sentences to be inserted into existing paragraphs and pictures to be placed to the right of related paragraphs. As you can see, the material has *topical relevance* (i.e., it is related to the topic of lightning) but it lacks *conceptual relevance* (i.e., it is not related to an explanation of the process of lightning formation).

Garner and her colleagues coined the term *seductive details* to refer to interesting but irrelevant material that is added to a passage to spice it up (Garner, Brown, Sanders, & Menke, 1992; Garner, Gillingham, & White, 1989). To distinguish between the use of words and the use of pictures, Harp and Mayer (1997, 1998) used the term *seductive text* to refer to interesting but irrelevant text that is added to a passage and the term *seductive illustrations* to refer to interesting but irrelevant illustrations that are added to a passage. The seductive text and seductive illustrations in Figure 7.2 are *interesting* because readers rate them as entertaining and interesting. The seductive text and seductive illustrations in Figure 7.2 are *irrelevant* because they are not related to the cause-and-effect explanation of how lightning works.

The Case for Adding Interesting Words and Pictures

The major theoretical justification for adding seductive details (such as the seductive text and seductive illustrations in Figure 7.2) is *arousal theory* – the idea that students learn better when they are emotionally aroused by the material. Weiner (1990, 1992) has shown how arousal theories dominated the field of motivation in the past, and Kintsch (1980) has referred to the idea as *emotional interest*. According to arousal theory, adding interesting but irrelevant material energizes learners so they pay more attention and learn more overall. In this case, emotion affects cognition; that is, a high level of enjoyment induced by the seductive details causes the learner to pay more attention and encode more material from the lesson. We can predict that students who learn from lessons containing seductive details will perform better on tests of retention and transfer than will students who learn without seductive details.

What's wrong with arousal theory? In spite of its commonsense approach, arousal theory is based on an outmoded view of learning as

Actual picture of
airplane being struck
by lightning

Metal airplanes conduct lightning, but
sustain little damage.

When the surface of the earth is warm, moist air near the earth's surface becomes heated and rises rapidly, producing an updraft. As the air in these updrafts cools, water vapor condenses into water droplets and forms a cloud. When flying through updrafts, an airplane ride can become bumpy. Metal airplanes conduct lightning very well, but they sustain little damage because the bolt, meeting no resistance, passes right through. The cloud's top extends above the freezing level. At this altitude, the air temperature is well below freezing, so the upper portion of the cloud is composed of tiny ice crystals.

Freezing level

Ice crystals

Water droplets

Updrafts

Warm moist air

Warm moist air rises, water vapor
condenses and forms a cloud.

Figure 7.2 A portion of a multimedia lesson on lightning with interesting but irrelevant words and pictures added.

information acquisition (as in the information-delivery theory of multi-media learning) – the idea that learning involves taking information from the teacher and putting it in the learner. In contrast, the cognitive theory of multimedia learning is based on the view of learning as *knowledge construction* – the idea that learners actively build mental representations based on what is presented and what they already know. It follows that seductive details may interfere with the process of knowledge construction, an idea spelled out in the next section.

The Case Against Adding Interesting Words and Pictures

In this classic book, *Interest and Effort in Education,* Dewey (1913) argued against viewing interest as an ingredient that could be added to spice up an otherwise boring lesson. In particular, Dewey noted: "When things have to be made interesting, it is because interest itself is wanting. Moreover, the phrase is a misnomer. The thing, the object, is no more interesting than it was before" (Dewey, 1913, pp. 11–12). More recently, Kintsch (1980) used the term *cognitive interest* to refer to the idea that students enjoy lessons that they can understand. According to this view, cognition affects emotion; that is, when students can make sense out of a lesson, they tend to enjoy the lesson.

In contrast to arousal theory, the cognitive theory of multimedia learning suggests that adding seductive details can interfere with the process of knowledge construction in several ways – involving selecting relevant information, organizing the information into a coherent structure, and integrating material with existing knowledge. First, the presence of seductive details may direct the learner's attention away from the relevant material about the steps in lightning formation. Second, the insertion of seductive details within the explanation may disrupt the learner's ability to build a cause-and-effect chain among the main steps in lightning formation. Third, the learners may assume that the theme of the passage comes from the seductive details – such as stories about people being injured by lightning – and therefore try to integrate all incoming information into a general framework about lightning injuries. Harp and Mayer (1998) provide some evidence favoring the third hypothesis, but additional research is needed. According to the cognitive theory of multimedia learning, adding seductive details will result in poorer performance on tests of retention and transfer.

Research on Coherence Principle 1

Does adding interesting but irrelevant words and/or pictures to a multimedia explanation affect student learning? To answer this question, my colleagues and I conducted six separate comparisons of the retention and transfer performance of students who received a basic version of a multimedia presentation like the one shown in Figure 7.1 with the performance of students who received an expanded version that also contained added words and/or pictures such as those shown in Figure 7.2 (Harp & Mayer, 1997, Experiment 1; Harp & Mayer, 1998, Experiments 1–4; Mayer, Heiser, & Lonn, in press, Experiment 1). Five of the tests involved a paper-based environment; one involved a computer-based environment. The retention test involved writing down an explanation for how lightning storms develop and the transfer test involved writing as many answers as possible to questions such as "How can you decrease the intensity of a lightning storm?" According to the interest hypothesis, adding interesting but irrelevant words and/or pictures should result in improved retention and transfer performance, whereas the cognitive theory of multimedia learning yields the opposite prediction.

Coherence Effects for Retention

Figure 7.3 shows the mean retention scores for students who received the basic version of the lesson (i.e., bars labeled "annotated illustrations" or "narrated animation") and those who received the expanded version (i.e., bars labeled "annotated illustrations with added details" or "narrated animation with added details"). In all cases, students who received the basic version remembered more steps in the process of lightning formation than did students who received the expanded version. I refer to this pattern as a *coherence effect for retention* because adding interesting material tended to hurt student learning. The coherence effect for retention (type 1) is that students perform more poorly on verbal retention when interesting but irrelevant words or pictures are added to a multimedia explanation. The effect sizes for this coherence effect, summarized in Figure 7.4, are consistent and strong, with a median of 2.37. Similarly, the percentage gain is also consistent and strong, with the learners who receive the basic version of the lesson remembering a median of 189% more of the important material than learners who receive the expanded version. Clearly, eliminating interesting but irrelevant material from a lesson helps students to better remember the remaining material. Importantly, the coherence effect for retention occurs both in paper-based and computer-based environments.

Coherence Effects for Transfer

Figure 7.5 shows the mean transfer scores for students who received a basic version (i.e., annotated illustrations or narrated animation) and

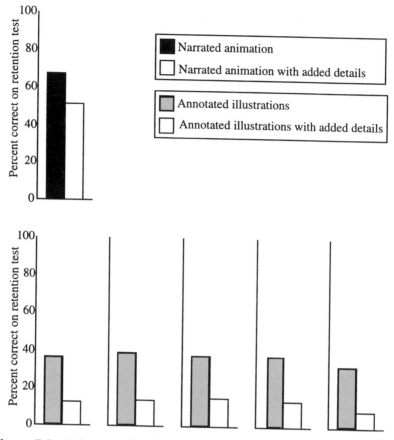

Figure 7.3 Coherence effect (type 1) for retention: better retention when interesting but irrelevant details are excluded (*dark bars*) rather than included (*white bars*).

Figure 7.4 Coherence Effect (Type 1) for Retention: Summary of Results

Source	Content	Context	Effect size	Percent gain
Mayer et al., in press, Exp. 1	Lightning	Screen	.65	35
Harp and Mayer, 1998, Exp. 1	Lightning	Page	2.82	194
Harp and Mayer, 1998, Exp. 2	Lightning	Page	2.31	184
Harp and Mayer, 1998, Exp. 3	Lightning	Page	1.98	151
Harp and Mayer, 1998, Exp. 4	Lightning	Page	2.44	199
Harp and Mayer, 1997, Exp. 1	Lightning	Page	3.63	322
Median			**2.37**	**189**

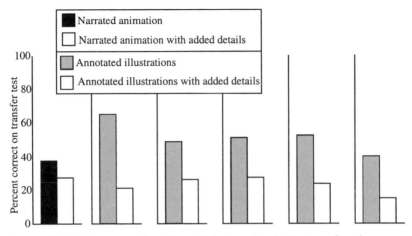

Figure 7.5 Coherence effect (type 1) for transfer: better transfer when interesting but irrelevant details are excluded (*dark bars*) rather than included (*white bars*).

for those who received an expanded version (i.e., annotated illustrations with added details and narrated animation with added details) of the multimedia lesson. In all cases, students who received a basic version generated more solutions to transfer problems than did students who received an expanded version. We call this pattern a *coherence effect for transfer* because adding interesting but irrelevant material resulted in poorer problem-solving transfer performance. Figure 7.6 shows that the coherence size effects are consistent and strong – with a median of 1.66 – and occur both in paper-based and in computer-based environments. In addition, Figure 7.6 shows that the percentage gains are consistent and strong, with learners who receive the base lesson generating 105% more creative solutions on the transfer test than do learners who receive the expanded lesson.

Figure 7.6 Coherence Effect (Type 1) for Transfer: Summary of Results

Source	Content	Context	Effect size	Percent gain
Mayer et al., in press, Exp. 1	Lightning	Screen	.55	34
Harp and Mayer, 1998, Exp. 1	Lightning	Page	2.59	174
Harp and Mayer, 1998, Exp. 2	Lightning	Page	1.65	90
Harp and Mayer, 1998, Exp. 3	Lightning	Page	1.17	82
Harp and Mayer, 1998, Exp. 4	Lightning	Page	1.85	121
Harp and Mayer, 1997, Exp. 1	Lightning	Page	1.67	167
Median			**1.66**	**105**

Overall, the first version of the coherence effect is consistent with the cognitive theory of multimedia learning and inconsistent with the arousal theory. In the case of adding interesting words and pictures, this research shows that less is more – that is, learning about how a system works can be deeper when less material is presented.

Related Research

In general, previous research on seductive details documents that adding interesting text that is irrelevant to the theme of a passage either reduces or does not enhance students' remembering of the main ideas in the passage (Garner et al., 1992; Garner et al., 1989; Hidi & Baird, 1988; Mohr, Glover, & Ronning, 1984; Shirey, 1992; Shirey & Reynolds, 1988; Wade, 1992; Wade & Adams, 1990). In addition, students tend to be able to remember the seductive details better than they can remember the central ideas in the passage (Garner, Alexander, Gillingham, Kulikowich, & Brown, 1991; Garner et al., 1992; Hidi & Anderson, 1992; Hidi & Baird, 1986). The current research goes beyond other research on seductive details by focusing on the role of seductive details in multimedia presentations – including text-based and computer-based environments – rather than in text passages alone, by examining the effects of adding interesting words and pictures rather than words alone, and by evaluating learning outcomes with retention and transfer tests rather than retention alone.

COHERENCE PRINCIPLE 2: STUDENT LEARNING IS HURT WHEN INTERESTING BUT IRRELEVANT SOUNDS AND MUSIC ARE ADDED TO A MULTIMEDIA PRESENTATION

Introduction

How Can We Improve Multimedia Presentations?

The foregoing section showed the detrimental effects of adding interesting but irrelevant words and pictures to a multimedia presentation. Our valiant effort to spice up the lesson failed – perhaps because the added material (i.e., words and pictures) was too much like the target material. Undaunted, let's try another way to make the lesson more interesting. Let's return to the concise narrated animation on lightning formation as summarized in Figure 2.2 and see if there is some other way to make it more enjoyable.

One tempting technique for making a multimedia lesson more interesting is to add some bells and whistles in the form of background music or environmental sounds. For example, we can add a short instrumental music loop that plays continuously in the background. The music does not interfere with the narration but provides a gentle musical background to the presentation. In addition, we can add environmental sounds that correspond to events in the process of lightning formation, such as the sound of blowing wind when the program mentions gusts of cool wind or the sound of ice cubes crackling when the program mentions the formation of ice crystals. Again, the environmental sounds do not interfere with the narration but rather provide appropriate sound effects for the presentation.

The Case for Adding Interesting Sounds and Music

The rationale for adding background music and sounds is based on arousal theory, similar to the rationale for adding interesting words and pictures. According to arousal theory, music and sound effects make the multimedia presentation more enjoyable to the learner, thereby increasing the learner's level of emotional arousal. This increase in arousal results in increased attention to the presented material and therefore to more learning. On the basis of arousal theory, we can predict that adding interesting music and sounds will result in improved performance on tests of retention and transfer.

What's wrong with this straightforward approach to improving multimedia presentations? As in the first section of this chapter, the major problem is that the rationale for adding interesting music and sounds is based on an outmoded view of learning as information acquisition. According to this view, information is simply transferred from teachers to learners, and background music and sounds can speed up this delivery process. However, my approach in this book is based on the knowledge-construction view of learning – the idea that learners seek to actively build mental representations that make sense. Unfortunately, adding music and sounds can interfere with this sense-making process; this hypothesis is examined in the next section.

The Case Against Adding Interesting Sounds and Music

According to the cognitive theory of multimedia learning, learners process multimedia messages in their visual and auditory channels, both of which are limited in capacity. In the case of a narrated animation, the animation is processed in the visual channel and the narration is processed in the auditory channel. As is shown in Figure 7.7, when additional auditory information is presented, it competes with the narration for limited processing capacity in the auditory channel. When

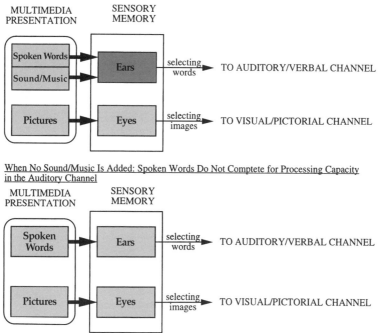

Figure 7.7 A cognitive analysis of how adding irrelevant sounds and music can disrupt learning: presentations with sound and music and without sound or music.

processing capacity is used to process the music and sounds, there is less capacity available for paying attention to the narration, organizing it into a coherent cause-and-effect chain, and linking it with the incoming visual information. On the basis of this theory, we can predict that adding interesting music and sounds to a multimedia presentation will result in poorer performance on tests of retention and transfer. In short, the cognitive theory of multimedia learning predicts a coherence effect in which adding interesting material – in the form of music and sounds – hurts student learning.

Research on Coherence Principle 2

Does adding interesting music and sounds to a multimedia explanation affect student learning and understanding? To answer this question, we conducted two separate comparisons of the retention and transfer performance of students who received a narrated animation with the performance of students who received an expanded version that also contained background music and environmental sounds (Moreno & Mayer, 2000, Experiments 1 and 2). Both tests involved a computer-based environment – one involved an explanation of lightning and the other involved an explanation of how car braking systems work. According to the arousal hypothesis, adding background music and sounds should result in improved retention and transfer performance, whereas the cognitive theory of multimedia learning yields the opposite prediction.

Coherence Effects for Retention

Figure 7.8 shows the mean retention scores for students who received the basic version of the lesson (i.e., narrated animation) and those who received the expanded version (i.e., narrated animation with sounds and music). In both cases, students who received the basic version remembered more steps in the process of lightning formation than did students who received the expanded version. As in the first section of this chapter, we refer to this pattern as a *coherence effect for retention* because adding interesting material tended to hurt student learning. The coherence effect for retention (type 2) is that students perform more poorly on verbal retention when background sounds and music are added to a multimedia explanation. The effect sizes for this coherence effect, summarized in Figure 7.9, are consistent and strong, with a median of 1.11. Additionally, Figure 7.9 shows that students given the basic version generated a median of

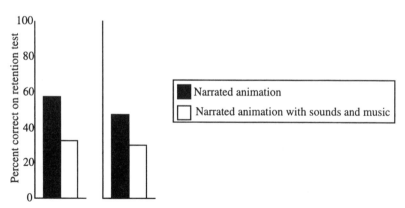

Figure 7.8 Coherence effect (type 2) for retention: better retention when interesting but irrelevant sounds and music are excluded (*dark bars*) rather than included (*white bars*).

Figure 7.9 Coherence Effect (Type 2) for Retention: Summary of Results

Source	Content	Context	Effect size	Percent gain
Moreno and Mayer, 2000, Exp 1	Lightning	Screen	1.27	77
Moreno and Mayer, 2000, Exp. 2	Brakes	Screen	.96	61
Median			**1.11**	**69**

69% more of the important material on the retention test than did students who received the expanded version.

Coherence Effects for Transfer

Figure 7.10 shows the mean transfer scores for students who received the basic version (i.e., narrated animation) and for those who received the expanded version (i.e., narrated animation with sounds and music) of the multimedia lesson. In both cases, students who received the basic version generated more solutions to transfer problems than did students who received the expanded version. We call this pattern a *coherence effect for transfer* because adding background music and sounds resulted in poorer problem-solving transfer performance. Figure 7.11 shows that the coherence size effects are consistent and strong – with a median of 1.23 – and are similar to those obtained for coherence principle 1. In addition, Figure 7.11 shows that students who received the basic version of the multime-

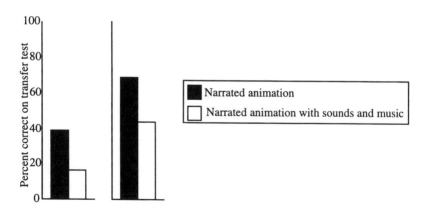

Figure 7.10 Coherence effect (type 2) for transfer: better transfer when interesting but irrelevant sounds and music are excluded (*dark bars*) rather than included (*white bars*).

Figure 7.11 Coherence Effect (Type 2) for Transfer: Summary of Results

Source	Content	Context	Effect size	Percent gain
Moreno and Mayer, 2000, Exp. 1	Lightning	Screen	1.56	149
Moreno and Mayer, 2000, Exp. 2	Brakes	Screen	.90	61
Median			**1.23**	**105**

dia lesson generated a median of 105% more creative solutions than did students who received the expanded version.

Overall, this second version of the coherence effect is consistent with the cognitive theory of multimedia learning and inconsistent with the arousal theory.

Related Research

Research on children's television examines how viewers' attention can be guided through the use of audio features (Anderson & Lorch, 1983; Kozma, 1991). For example, sound effects generally cause children to pay attention – albeit momentarily – to a TV presentation (Alwitt, Anderson, Lorch, & Levin, 1980; Calvert & Scott, 1989). Kozma (1991, p. 194) summarizes this line research as follows: "This research paints a picture of television viewers who monitor a presentation at a low level of engagement, their moment-to-moment visual attention periodically attracted by salient audio cues…" As you can see, this line of research does not focus on multimedia learning situations like the ones we studied, but it does suggest that auditory features of a presentation may guide the learner's attention toward specific content.

COHERENCE PRINCIPLE 3: STUDENT LEARNING IS IMPROVED WHEN UNNEEDED WORDS ARE REMOVED FROM A MULTIMEDIA PRESENTATION

Introduction

How Can We Improve Multimedia Presentations?

In the first two sections of this chapter, we attempted to spice up a multimedia lesson by adding interesting words and pictures or by adding background music and sound effects. In both cases, the added material, which was intended to improve the multimedia lesson, turned out to hurt student learning and understanding. The theme of our results, which we call a coherence effect, is that students are better able to make sense out of a multimedia lesson when interesting but irrelevant material is not included.

In this section, we take this less-is-more theme one step further. Let's begin with a text passage and captioned illustrations such as those shown in Figure 7.1. The text passage contains approximately 500 words, many of which are not directly relevant to the theme of the lesson – namely, a description of the steps in the cause-and-effect chain leading to lightning formation. In fact, the central steps from the text are reproduced in the captions of the illustrations. To make the lesson more concise, we could eliminate the text passage and present learners with only the captioned illustrations. The captioned illustrations constitute a highly concentrated summary of the main steps in lightning formation, presented both in words and pictures.

The Case for Retaining Unneeded Words

At first blush, it seems obvious that students will learn more from a full presentation than from a summary. The theoretical rationale is straightforward: In the full version, the words describing the steps in lightning formation are presented twice – within the text passage in elaborated form and within the captions in abbreviated form. In the summary version, the words describing the steps in lightning formation are presented only once – within the captions. Two ways of delivering the words are better than one, so students should learn more in the full presentation than in the summary presentation. This argument is consistent with the information-delivery hypothesis – namely, the idea that students learn more when they receive information via more routes.

The Case Against Retaining Unneeded Words

Why would a summary result in better learning than the full presentation would? According to the cognitive theory of multimedia learning, learners actively make sense out of the presented material by selecting relevant information, organizing it into a coherent representation, and linking it with other knowledge. The summary greatly facilities this process because the key words are in the captions, they are presented in order, and they are presented near the corresponding illustration. Thus, the cognitive processes involved in sense making can be facilitated by a clear and concise summary. This argument is consistent with the cognitive theory of multimedia learning. On the basis of this theory, we can predict that students given a multimedia summary will perform as well or better on tests of retention and transfer than will students given the summary along with the regular text passage.

Research on Coherence Principle 3

Do students learn better from a multimedia summary than from a full lesson? In the case of the lightning passage, the multimedia summary (i.e., annotated illustrations) presents a concise statement of the cause-and-effect chain in words and illustrations, as in the captioned illustrations on the left side of Figure 7.1. The full lesson (i.e., annotated illustrations with added text) contains the same captioned illustrations along with approximately 550 words of text, as shown in Figure 7.1. In three studies, we compared the retention and transfer performance of students who read a multimedia summary with the performance of students who read a full lesson on lightning (Mayer, Bove, Bryman, Mars, & Tapangco, 1996, Experiments 1 through 3).

Coherence Effects for Retention

Figure 7.12 shows the mean retention scores for students who received the summary version of the lesson (i.e., annotated illustrations) and those who received the full version (i.e., annotated illustrations with added text). In three of three cases, students who received the summary version remembered more steps in the process of lightning formation (i.e., material emphasized in the captions of the annotated illustrations) than did students who received the full version. We refer to this pattern as a *coherence effect for retention* because deleting extraneous words tended to help student learning. The coherence effect for retention (type 3) is that students perform better on verbal retention when extraneous words are removed from a multimedia explanation. The effect sizes for this coherence effect, summarized in Figure 7.13, are consistent and strong, with a median of 1.47. Figure 7.13 also shows that students given the summary version

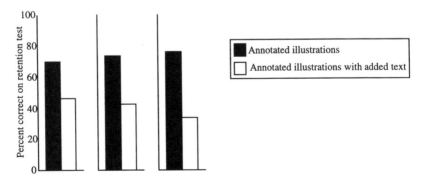

Figure 7.12 Coherence effect (type 3) for retention: equivalent or better retention when nonessential text is excluded (*dark bars*) rather than included (*white bars*).

Figure 7.13 Coherence Effect (Type 3) for Retention: Summary of Results

Source	Content	Context	Effect size	Percent gain
Mayer et al., 1996, Exp. 1	Lightning	Page	1.47	51
Mayer et al., 1996, Exp. 2	Lightning	Page	.93	69
Mayer et al., 1996, Exp. 3	Lightning	Page	2.31	126
Median			**1.47**	**69**

generated a median of 69% more of the important material on the retention test than did students who received the full version.

Coherence Effects for Transfer

Figure 7.14 shows the mean transfer scores for students who received the summary (i.e., annotated illustrations) and for those who received full versions (i.e., annotated illustrations with added text) of the multimedia lesson. In all cases, students who received the summary version generated more solutions to transfer problems than did students who received the full version. We call this pattern a *coherence effect for transfer* because removing extraneous text resulted in improved problem-solving transfer performance. Figure 7.15 shows that the coherence effect sizes are consistent and moderate, with a median of .70, and students who received the summary version of the multimedia lesson generated a median of 28% more creative solutions than did students who received the full version.

Overall, this third version of the coherence effect is consistent with the cognitive theory of multimedia learning and inconsistent with arousal theory.

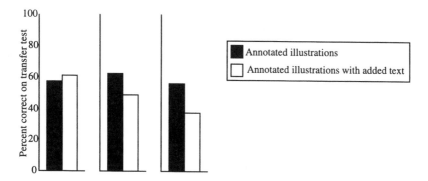

Figure 7.14 Coherence effect (type 3) for transfer: equivalent or better transfer when nonessential text is excluded (*dark bars*) rather than included (*white bars*).

Figure 7.15   Coherence Effect (Type 3) for Transfer: Summary of Results

Source	Content	Context	Effect size	Percent gain
Mayer et al., 1996, Exp 1	Lightning	Page	–.17	–6
Mayer et al., 1996, Exp. 2	Lightning	Page	.70	28
Mayer et al., 1996, Exp. 3	Lightning	Page	.98	50
Median			**.70**	**28**

Related Research

Our findings are consistent with earlier research showing that college students remember more important material from reading chapter summaries than from reading entire textbook chapters (Reder & Anderson, 1980). However, our research extends earlier work by also examining students' problem-solving transfer performance. Thus, our research shows not only that students remember more of the important material when it is presented as a summary but that they also better understand the material.

IMPLICATIONS

Implications for Multimedia Learning

The overarching theme of research on coherence is that adding interesting but irrelevant words or pictures to a lesson can sometimes result in poorer learning and understanding. In short, in the case of multimedia lessons, students tend to learn more when less is presented. The cognitive theory of multimedia learning helps to explain this apparent paradox. Learners are actively trying to make sense of the presented material by building a coherent mental representation, so adding extraneous information gets in the way of this structure-building process. Given the limits on working memory, cognitive resources must be diverted to process the irrelevant material and therefore are not available for processing the central material. In addition, when extraneous information is highly salient, learners may organize incoming material around the theme of the extraneous material – such as lightning injuries – rather than the author's intended theme – such as a cause-and-effect explanation of lightning formation.

Implications for Multimedia Design

The implications for multimedia design are clear: (1) do not add extraneous words and pictures to a multimedia presentation; (2) do not add unneeded sounds and music to a multimedia presentation; (3) keep the presentation short and to the point. A concise presentation allows the learner to build a coherent mental representation – that is, to focus on the key elements and mentally organize them in a way that makes sense. In short, our results show that multimedia designers should resist the temptation to add unneeded bells and whistles to an instructional presentation. The coherence design guideline is to avoid seemingly interesting words, pictures, and sounds that are not relevant to the lesson's main conceptual message. Needed elaboration should be presented after the learner has constructed a coherent mental representation of the basic cause-and-effect system. For example, after a concise multimedia presentation helps the learner understand the major steps in the process of lightning, additional material can be presented to elaborate on each step.

SUGGESTED READINGS

Coherence Principle 1: Student Learning Is Hurt When Interesting but Irrelevant Words and Pictures Are Added to a Multimedia Presentation

*Harp, S. F., & Mayer, R. E. (1998). How seductive details do their damage: A theory of cognitive interest in science learning. *Journal of Educational Psychology, 90,* 414–434.

*Harp, S. F., & Mayer, R. E. (1997). The role of interest in learning from scientific text and illustrations: On the distinction between emotional interest and cognitive interest. *Journal of Educational Psychology, 89,* 92–102.

*Mayer, R. E., Heiser, J., & Lonn, S. (in press). Cognitive constraints on multimedia learning: When presenting more material results in less understanding. *Journal of Educational Psychology.*

Coherence Principle 2: Student Learning Is Hurt When Interesting but Irrelevant Sounds and Music Are Added to a Multimedia Presentation

*Moreno, R., & Mayer, R. E. (2000). A coherence effect in multimedia learning: The case for minimizing irrelevant sounds in the design of multimedia messages. *Journal of Educational Psychology, 92,* 117–125.

Coherence Principle 3: Student Learning Is Improved When Unneeded Words Are Eliminated from a Multimedia Presentation

*Mayer, R. E., Bove, W., Bryman, A., Mars, R., & Tapangco, L. (1996). When less is more: Meaningful learning from visual and verbal summaries of science textbook lessons. *Journal of Educational Psychology, 88,* 64–73.

---

* Asterisk indicates that a portion of the chapter is based on this publication.

Modality Principle

Modality Principle: Students learn better from animation and narration than from animation and on-screen text; that is, students learn better when words in a multimedia message are presented as spoken text rather than printed text.

Theoretical Rationale: When pictures and words are both presented visually (i.e., as animation and text), the visual/pictorial channel can become overloaded but the auditory/verbal channel is unused. When words are presented auditorily, they can be processed in the auditory/verbal channel, thereby leaving the visual/pictorial channel to process only the pictures.

Empirical Rationale: In four of four tests, learners who received animation and narration performed better on tests of retention than did learners who received animation and on-screen text. In four of four tests, learners who received animation and narration performed better on tests of transfer than did learners who received animation and on-screen text.

■■ Chapter Outline

134

INTRODUCTION

Does Modality Matter?

Suppose you wanted to design a multimedia lesson to be presented via a computer system. Suppose the lesson involves a scientific explanation such as how car brakes work, how pumps work, or how lightning storms develop. Furthermore, suppose your goal is to help learners understand the explanation so that they will be able to answer problem-solving transfer questions that require applying the presented material to new situations. How would you proceed? So far, the research presented in this book yields several seemingly relevant principles: the multimedia principle – using words and pictures rather than words alone; the spatial contiguity principle – placing printed words near corresponding pictures; the temporal contiguity principle – presenting words and corresponding pictures at the same time; and the coherence principle – avoiding unneeded adjuncts.

For example, to construct a multimedia presentation on lightning formation, you develop a short animation depicting the major steps in the development of a lightning storm and you develop a short script that describes the steps in words. Consistent with the multimedia principle, you use both words (i.e., your script) and pictures (i.e., your animation). To comply with the temporal contiguity principle, you present each segment of the verbal script along with the corresponding portion of the animation. In light of the coherence principle, you write the script in a way that minimizes unneeded text. The resulting presentation can be called a *concise narrated animation* (CNA).

In designing your multimedia lesson on the basis of the multimedia, temporal contiguity, and coherence principles, you have to make a decision concerning the best way to present the words: You can present them as on-screen text (i.e., printed words) or as narration (i.e., spoken words). In both cases, the words are presented at the same time as the corresponding portion of the animation, but your decision in this chapter concerns whether to present the words in spoken or printed form. Figure 2.2 presents selected frames from a multimedia lesson on lightning along with concurrent narration indicated in quotation marks underneath each corresponding frame. I refer to this as a narrated animation. As an alternative, you could incorporate the words as on-screen text and present them at the bottom of the screen. To ensure equivalency, you present each of the sixteen segments of on-screen text for the same period that the corresponding narration segment was presented. This offers an alternative to a narrated animation, which I call a captioned animation. The top portion of Figure 8.1 presents a frame and corresponding narration segment from a narrated animation, whereas the bottom portion of Figure 8.1 presents a frame and corresponding on-screen text segment for a captioned animation.

Words as Narration

A

"As the air in this updraft cools, water vapor condenses into water droplets and forms a cloud."

Words as On-Screen Text

B

As the air in this updraft cools, water vapor condenses into water droplets and forms a cloud.

Figure 8.1 Frames of animation on lightning with **(A)** words as narration or **(B)** words as on-screen text.

Does modality matter? Is learning the same when words are presented as speech (e.g., the top of Figure 8.1) as when words are presented as on-screen text (e.g., the bottom of Figure 8.1)? Is one modality better than the other? This issue is explored in the next two sections.

Modality Does Not Matter: The Case for Expressing Words as On-Screen Text or Narration

The most straightforward approach is to assume that modality does not matter, so words can be presented either as on-screen text or as narration. The rationale for the claim that modality does not matter comes from the *information-delivery theory* – the idea that multimedia learning is improved by presenting information to learners via as many routes as possible. In the case of narrated animations, two delivery paths are used – words are delivered to the learner and pictures are delivered to the learner. In the case of captioned animations, two delivery paths are used – again both words and pictures are delivered to the learner. According to this view, learning should be the same for both multimedia presentations because the same information is presented to the learners.

The information-delivery theory is represented in Figure 8.2. The top panel shows two delivery paths, one for pictures and one for words (which happen to be spoken). The bottom frame also shows two delivery paths, one for pictures and one for words (which happen to be printed). When identical information is presented in the same temporal manner, the resulting learning outcome will be the same. The premise underlying the information-delivery theory is that learners need to receive verbal and visual information (i.e., words and pictures); obviously, pictures are presented visually, but the modality of the words does not matter because they have the same informational value when expressed as speech as when expressed as printed text. Therefore, the information-delivery theory predicts that learners who receive a multimedia lesson with words presented as on-screen text will perform the same on retention and transfer tests as learners who receive the identical lesson with words presented as narration. A more extreme version of the information-delivery theory predicts that on-screen text will result in better learning than narration because on-screen text can be reread whereas spoken text is fleeting.

Modality Matters: The Case for Expressing Words as Narration Rather Than as On-Screen Text

What's wrong with the information-delivery theory? It is based on an outmoded conception of learning as information acquisition in which learning involves taking presented information and placing it inside

Animation With Narration: Two Delivery Paths to The Learner

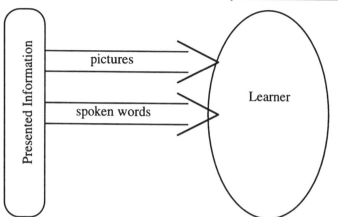

Animation With On-Screen Text: Two Delivery Paths to The Learner

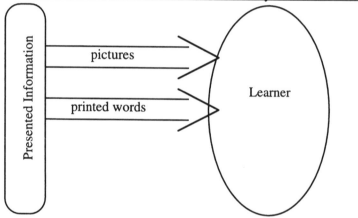

Figure 8.2 Why the information-delivery theory predicts no difference between captioned animation and narrated animation: **(A)** animation with narration; **(B)** animation with on-screen text.

one's memory. According to this conception, learning occurs when information is presented by the instructor and received by the student. It follows that in this view, the main concern of a multimedia designer is to present information to the learner. Although this view seems to be consistent with common sense, it conflicts with our current understanding of how the human mind works. In particular, it conflicts with what we know about dual-channel processing as described under the cognitive theory of multimedia learning in chapter 3.

The case for the idea that modality matters is based on the *cognitive theory of multimedia learning* and, in particular, its dual-channel assumption: People have two separate information-processing channels – one for visual/pictorial processing and one for auditory/verbal processing. When words are presented as narration, the auditory/verbal channel can be used for processing words (i.e., the narration) and the visual/pictorial channel can be used for processing pictures (i.e., the animation). In this way, the load is balanced between two channels, so neither one is excessively overloaded. This situation is depicted in the top frame of Figure 8.3, in which pictures enter through the eyes (and are processed in the visual/pictorial channel) while spoken words enter through the ears (and are processed in the auditory/verbal channel).

In contrast, when words are presented as on-screen text, the visual/pictorial channel is used at least initially for processing words (i.e., the on-screen text) and the visual/pictorial channel is used for processing

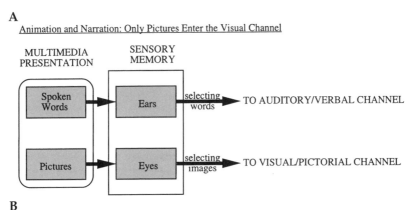

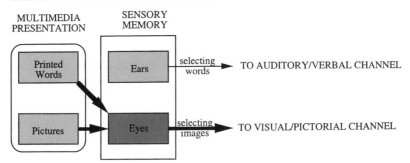

Figure 8.3 Why the cognitive theory of multimedia learning predicts differences between **(A)** narrated animation and **(B)** captioned animation.

pictures (i.e., the animation). At the same time, the auditory/verbal channel is not being used much at all. Each channel has limited capacity, so each can process only a limited amount of material at one time, meaning that one channel is overloaded with processing both words and pictures while the other channel is relatively underused. This situation is depicted in the bottom frame of Figure 8.3, in which both pictures and printed words must enter the learner's information processing through the eyes and initially be represented as images in working memory; thus, both compete for resources within the visual channel.

According to the cognitive theory of multimedia learning, the processes required for meaningful learning cannot be fully carried when the visual channel is overloaded – that is, when pictures and printed words compete for limited cognitive resources in the visual channel because both enter the information processing through the eyes. In contrast, the most efficient way to present verbal material is through the verbal channel – that is, as spoken text – because in this way it does not compete with pictures for cognitive resources in the visual channel. Instead, processing of words is off-loaded onto the verbal channel, which is otherwise underused. This theory predicts a *modality effect* in which presenting words as on-screen text rather than narration will result in poorer learning, as indicated by the results of retention tests, and in poorer understanding, as indicated by the results of transfer tests.

Understanding the Modality Effect

Mousavi, Low, and Sweller (1995, p. 321) used the term *modality effect* to refer to the idea that "effective cognitive capacity may be increased if both auditory and visual working memory can be used" to process incoming multimedia messages. In short, "effective size of working memory can be increased by presenting information in a mixed (auditory and visual mode) rather than a single mode" (Mousavi et al., 1995, p. 320). Mousavi et al. used the term *modality effect* in a broad sense to include situations in which presenting simultaneous visual and auditory material is superior to presenting the same material successively, – a result that I call the *contiguity effect*. In the view of Mousavi et al., modality effects are examples of *split attention* – a broader class of multimedia learning situations in which visual attention must be allocated to both pictorial and verbal material. In contrast, Moreno and Mayer (1999) use the term *modality effect* in a more restricted sense to refer only to situations in which presenting pictures and spoken text (e.g., animation and narration) is more effective than presenting pictures and printed text (e.g., animation and on-screen text). I use this more restricted definition of modality effect in this book.

A fundamental theoretical idea underlying the modality effect is dual-channel processing – the idea that there are separate channels for processing visually presented material and auditorily presented material. For example, Baddeley's (1992) model of working memory includes a distinction between a *visuo-spatial sketch pad* that is used for processing visual material and a *phonological loop* that is used for processing auditory material. Paivio's (1986) dual-coding theory makes a somewhat similar distinction. A second fundamental theoretical idea underlying the modality effect is limited capacity – the idea that each channel is limited in the amount of processing it can support at one time. Finally, a third fundamental theoretical idea is active learning – the idea that meaningful learning occurs when a learner selects, organizes, and integrates knowledge in each channel. These processes require cognitive capacity and therefore are restricted when one or both channels are overloaded.

RESEARCH ON MODALITY

Does modality matter? Does it matter whether words in a multimedia message are presented in printed or spoken form, as long as the same verbal information is presented? To answer this question, we conducted a set of four studies in which we compared the retention and transfer performance of students who received a narrated animation or the same animation along with concurrent on-screen text explaining how lightning storms develop (Mayer & Moreno, 1998, Experiment 1; Moreno & Mayer, 1999, Experiments 1 and 2) or how car braking systems work (Mayer & Moreno, 1998). The top of Figure 8.1 exemplifies a portion of the narrated animation treatment (animation with narration), whereas the bottom of Figure 8.1 exemplifies a portion of the animation with on-screen text treatment (animation with text). The retention test involved writing down an explanation for how lightning storms develop (or how car brakes work) and was scored by tallying the number of essential steps that were recalled. The transfer test involved writing answers to such essay questions as "What could be done to reduce the intensity of a lightning storm?" (for the lightning lesson) or "What could be done to make brakes more reliable – that is, to make sure they would not fail?" (for the brakes lesson) and was scored by tallying the total number of acceptable answers. According to the information-delivery theory, students who receive the animation-with-narration treatment and those who receive the animation-with-text treatment should perform equivalently on tests of retention and transfer, but the cognitive theory of multimedia learning predicts

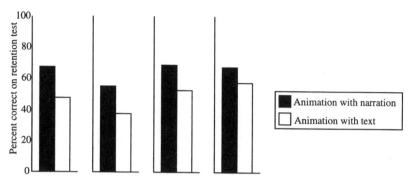

Figure 8.4 Modality effect for retention: better retention when words are presented as narration (*dark bars*) rather than as on-screen text (*white bars*).

superior retention and transfer performance for students who receive the animation-with-narration treatment.

Modality Effect for Retention

Figure 8.4 shows the mean retention scores for students who received the animation-with-narration and animation-with-text treatments. In all four cases, animation-with-narration students remembered more of the steps in the process of lightning formation than did animation-with-text students. We refer to this pattern as a *modality effect for retention* because using on-screen text with animation reduced student learning in comparison to using narration with animation. The modality effect for retention is that students perform more poorly on verbal retention when they learn with animation and text than when they learn with animation and narration. The effect sizes for this modality effect, summarized in Figure 8.5, are consistent and moderately strong, with a median of .84. The percentage improvement in retention performance for the animation-with-narration students over the animation-with-text students is also consistent and moderately strong, with a median of 30%; that is, the animation-with-narration students remem-

Figure 8.5 Modality Effect for Retention: Summary of Results

Source	Content	Effect size	Percent gain
Moreno and Mayer, in press, Exp. 1	Lightning	1.00	27
Moreno and Mayer, in press, Exp. 2	Lightning	.80	47
Mayer and Moreno, 1998, Exp. 1	Lightning	.89	33
Mayer and Moreno, 1998, Exp. 2	Brakes	.48	17
Median		**.84**	**30**

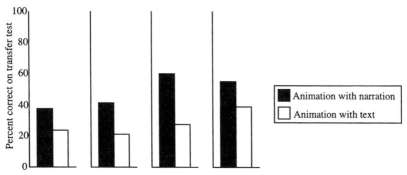

Figure 8.6 Modality effect for transfer: better transfer when words are presented as narration (*dark bars*) rather than as on-screen text (*white bars*).

bered on average 30% more of the important material than did the animation-with-text students.

Modality Effect for Transfer

Figure 8.6 shows the mean transfer scores for students who received the animation-with-narration and animation-with-text treatments. In four of four comparisons, animation-with-narration students generated more solutions to transfer problems than did animation-with-text students. We refer to this pattern as a *modality effect for transfer* because using on-screen text instead of narration tends to hurt student understanding of a multimedia presentation. In short, the modality effect is that students perform more poorly on problem-solving transfer when they learn with narration and animation than when they learn with narration and animation. The modality effect sizes, summarized in Figure 8.7, are consistent and strong, with a median of 1.17. In addition, the percentage gain on transfer of the animation-with-narration students over the animation-with-text group is consistent and strong, with a median of 80%; that is, the animation-with-narration students generated on average 80% more creative solutions on the transfer test than did the animation-with-text students.

Figure 8.7 Modality Effect for Transfer: Summary of Results

Source	Content	Effect size	Percent gain
Moreno and Mayer, 1999, Exp. 1	Lightning	1.06	65
Moreno and Mayer, 1999, Exp. 2	Lightning	1.28	95
Mayer and Moreno, 1998, Exp. 1	Lightning	1.68	114
Mayer and Moreno, 1998, Exp. 2	Brakes	.94	41
Median		**1.17**	**80**

Overall, the modality effect is consistent with the cognitive theory of multimedia learning and inconsistent with the information-delivery theory. Indeed, the results provide overwhelming evidence that modality matters.

Related Research

Although the studies reported above are the first to discover a modality effect involving computer-based multimedia messages, a similar effect has been identified for book-based multimedia messages (Mousavi et al., 1995). For example, Mousavi et al. (1995) presented students with worked-out examples for how to solve various geometry problems. Some students viewed a printed diagram (on a sheet of paper) while listening to a tape recording that explained the solution in words (narration and illustration), whereas other students viewed a printed diagram and viewed printed statements identical to the tape-recorded words (printed text and illustration). The results across several studies revealed a modality effect in which presenting words in spoken form resulted in better performance on a geometry test than did presenting the words in printed form. The results of our research complement and extend this finding by demonstrating a modality effect in computer-based multimedia environments and by using a rich set of dependent measures that assessed both retention and transfer.

IMPLICATIONS

Implications for Multimedia Learning

In four separate tests, we began with a concise narrated animation which provided a scientific explanation and found that learning was hurt when we substituted on-screen text for the narration. We refer to this finding as a *modality effect*: Substituting on-screen text for narration detracts from multimedia learning,

On the surface, the results seem to conflict with common sense. The on-screen text and the narration contained the same words, so both treatment groups received identical information – the same words and the same pictures. The only difference was that one group received the words as text (animation-with-text group) and one group received the words as narration (animation-with-narration group). Clearly, there is something wrong with the commonsense view that student learning will be equivalent when students are presented with the same information (or the more extreme notion that printed text – which can be reread – is better than spoken text –

which is fleeting). This prediction is based on what we call the infor-mation-delivery theory – the idea that the amount of learning depends on the amount of information that is delivered to the learner. To understand the modality effect, it is necessary to move beyond the information-delivery theory to consider a cognitive the-ory of how people process multimedia material.

These results are most consistent with a cognitive theory of multi-media learning that posits dual information processing channels. When a concise narrated animation is presented, the pictures (i.e., animation) are processed in the visual channel while the words (i.e., narration) are processed in the auditory channel. However, when we present the words as on-screen text rather than as narration, both the words and pictures must be processed – at least initially – through the visual channel. The visual system is more likely to become over-loaded for the animation-and-text presentation than for the anima-tion-and-narration presentation, resulting in less learning and understanding.

Although on-screen text proved to be detrimental in this research, it does not follow that all instances of printed text should be avoided. Our research on the spatial contiguity effect in chapter 5, for exam-ple, found that students learn better when illustrations and corre-sponding printed text occur near rather than far from each other on a page or screen. In these cases, students seem to have engaged in meaningful learning from printed words and illustrations.

What is the relationship between the spatial contiguity effect and the modality effect? In the spatial contiguity effect, presenting text and pictures can result in meaningful learning, whereas in the modality effect, presenting text and pictures results in poorer learn-ing. First, the spatial contiguity effect compares placing text near the corresponding part of the illustration (or animation) to placing text far from it. According to a cognitive theory of multimedia learning, placing text near the picture it describes increases the chances that the learner will be able to make mental connections between corre-sponding words and pictures. Second, the modality effect compares presenting animation and narration with presenting animation and text – when the text is placed far from the corresponding part of the animation. Consistent with the spatial contiguity effect, the anima-tion-and-text group performs poorly on retention and transfer. In both the spatial contiguity effect and the modality effect, the key to meaningful learning is fostering appropriate cognitive processing, such as making mental connections between corresponding words and pictures. In both studies, learning is hurt when printed words are placed far from the pictures they describe.

Implications for Multimedia Design

The modality effect suggests an important design principle: When making a multimedia presentation consisting of animation and words, present the words as narration rather than as on-screen text. It is important to note that this design principle has been demonstrated in situations in which the animated narration runs at a fast rate without learner control of the presentation.

There may be situations in which printed text can foster meaningful learning, especially when it is used in a way that is consistent with the spatial contiguity principle. Therefore, the modality effect should not be used to justify a blanket prescription to never present printed text and animation together. Instead, multimedia design decisions should be based on an understanding of how people process information – such as the cognitive theory of multimedia learning – rather than on a set of blindly followed rules. Presenting words in printed form may be harmful in some situations – such as in the studies described in this chapter – but not in other situations – such as demonstrated for the spatial contiguity effect in chapter 3.

In answer to the question "Does modality matter?" research on the modality principle consistently demonstrates that the answer is yes – at least in the kinds of situations we examined in this chapter. Words as text and words as narration may be processed differently by learners even when the words are identical. Adding the research reviewed in this chapter with that found in the previous ones, I can conclude that the best way to present words and animated pictures in a computer-based environment with fixed speed of presentation is as a concise narrated animation.

SUGGESTED READINGS

*Mayer, R. E., & Moreno, R. (1998). A split-attention effect in multimedia learning: Evidence for dual processing systems in working memory. *Journal of Educational Psychology, 90,* 312–320.

Mousavi, S., Low, R., & Sweller, J. (1995). Reducing cognitive load by mixing auditory and visual presentation modes. *Journal of Educational Psychology, 87,* 319–334.

*Moreno, R., & Mayer, R. E. (1999). Cognitive principles of multimedia learning: The role of modality and contiguity. *Journal of Educational Psychology, 91,* 358–368.

---

* Asterisk indicates that part of the chapter is based on this publication.

9

Redundancy Principle

Redundancy Principle: Students learn better from animation and narration than from animation, narration, and text.

Theoretical Rationale: When pictures and words are both presented visually (i.e., as animation and text), the visual channel can become overloaded.

Empirical Rationale: In two of two tests, learners who received narration and animation performed better on tests of retention than did learners who received animation, narration, and text. In two of two tests, learners who received narration and animation performed better on tests of transfer than did learners who received animation, narration, and text.

■■ Chapter Outline

INTRODUCTION

How Can We Improve Concise Narrated Animations?

Suppose there is a multimedia encyclopedia that contains entries based on the principles outlined so far in this book. For example, for each scientific explanation in the encyclopedia – such as how car brakes work, how the pumps work, or how lightning storms develop – the computer presents a short animation depicting the main steps in the process along with concurrent narration describing the main steps in the process. Thus, the multimedia explanations consist of *concise narrated animations* (or CNAs). *Concise* refers to a focus on the essential steps in the process; *narrated* refers to the words being presented as speech; and *animations* refers to the pictures being presented as an animation. The top of Figure 9.1 shows a selected frame from a concise narrated ani-

Animation with Narration

A

"As the air in this updraft cools, water vapor condenses into water droplets and forms a cloud."

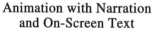

Animation with Narration and On-Screen Text

As the air in this updraft cools, water vapor condenses into water droplets and forms a cloud.

B

"As the air in this updraft cools, water vapor condenses into water droplets and forms a cloud."

Figure 9.1   Frame from lightning lesson with **(A)** animation and narration or with **(B)** animation, narration, and on-screen text.

mation for lightning formation: As the animation segment containing this frame appears on the screen, the spoken words shown in the quotation marks come out of the speakers (or headphones).

What can be done to improve on the concise narrated animations that have been created, that is, to help all students understand the explanations? One seemingly helpful suggestion is to add on-screen text that corresponds to the narration. An example is shown in the bottom of Figure 9.1. In this case, the narrated animation of lightning formation is augmented with on-screen text presented at the bottom of the screen. The on-screen text contains the same words as in the narration, and each sentence is on the screen during the same period that the corresponding narration is being spoken.

The Case for Adding On-Screen Text to Narrated Animations

The rationale for adding on-screen text to concise narrated animations is based on what can be called the *learning-preferences hypothesis*: Different people learn in different ways, so it is best to present information in many different formats. For example, if a student prefers to learn from spoken words, the student can pay attention to the narration; if another student prefers to learn from printed words, that student can pay attention to the on-screen text. By using multiple presentation formats, instructors can accommodate each student's preferred learning style. As you can see, the learning preferences hypothesis is based on the information delivery theory of multimedia learning.

The learning preferences hypothesis is represented in Figure 9.2. The top frame shows just one delivery path from the presented information to the learner, so information may have a hard time getting through. Even worse, the one available path may be blocked if the learner is not efficient in processing material in that form. When two paths are available, as shown in the middle frame, more information can get to the learner; if there is a blockage in one path, information can still get through on the other. However, there still may be some blockage in the flow of incoming information if the learner is unable to use one of the paths. For example, the spoken-word path may be blocked if the learner is not efficient in processing auditory information. The bottom frame shows three delivery paths from the presented material to the learner; this arrangement allows the learner to receive more information than does using just two paths. Importantly, the information can get through even if some of the paths are blocked; if the spoken-word path is blocked (such as for learners who are inefficient in auditory processing), verbal information can still get through via the printed-word path, and if the printed-word path is blocked (such as for learners who

A <u>Narration Only: One Delivery Path to The Learner</u>

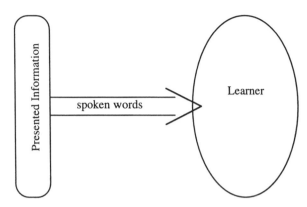

B

<u>Narrated Animation: Two Delivery Paths to The Learner</u>

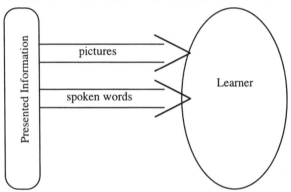

C <u>Narrated Animation with Redundant Text: Three Delivery Paths to The Learner</u>

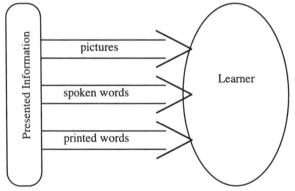

Figure 9.2 Why the information-delivery hypothesis predicts that a combination of animation, narration, and on-screen text **(C)** is better than animation with narration only **(B)** or **(A)** narration alone.

150

are poor at visual processing), verbal information can still get through via the spoken-word path. Another way of making the same point is to apply a straightforward interpretation of the information-delivery hypothesis: Adding a third form of presentation increases learning by offering another delivery route.

The role of individual differences in learning has long been recognized in educational psychology (Cronbach & Snow, 1977; Jonassen & Grabowski, 1993). For example, Jonassen and Grabowski (1993, p. xii) have shown how "individual differences are learning filters." In the case of the multimedia explanations, students who prefer auditory learning will have difficulty if material is presented solely as printed text, and students who prefer text-based learning will have difficulty if material is presented solely as narration. One solution to this problem is to adapt instruction to better fit the ways that individual students learn: "It is possible and desirable to adapt the nature of instruction to accommodate differences in ability, style, or preferences among individuals to improve learning outcomes" (Jonassen & Grabowski, 1993, p. 19). When customized lessons are not feasible, a possible alternative is to incorporate multiple instructional methods and formats into a single lesson. Thus, the suggestion to present words as both narration and on-screen text is a somewhat modest implementation of this general principle.

The premise underlying the learning-style hypothesis is that learners should be allowed to choose the method of instruction that best suits the way they learn, including being able to choose the format in which information is presented. If the same material is presented in many formats, such as pictures, printed text, and spoken text, then learners can focus on the format that best suits their learning preferences. When a student's preferred presentation mode is not included, that student will have more difficulty in learning – consistent with the *learning-filter* metaphor. On the basis of this theory, we can predict that adding on-screen text to a concise animated narration will result in improved learning, as measured by tests of retention, and in improved understanding, as measured by tests of transfer.

The Case Against Adding On-Screen Text to Narrated Animations

What's wrong with the learning-preferences hypothesis? At the most fundamental level, it is based on the information-delivery theory of multimedia learning in which learning is viewed as transmitting information from the teacher to the learner. According to this concept, learning occurs when information is presented by the instructor and received by the student. It follows that the reception will be better when more rather than fewer delivery paths are used, particularly in case some of the paths are blocked. This view conflicts with the cognitive theory of multimedia learning, presented in chapter 3, in which learners actively build mental representations within their information processing systems.

The case against adding on-screen text is based on the *capacity-limitation hypothesis*: People have limited capacity to process visually presented material and limited capacity to process auditorily presented material. The limited-capacity hypothesis is based on the cognitive theory of multimedia learning described in chapter 3 and is summarized in Figure 9.3. When words are presented visually – as on-screen text – this places an additional load on the visual information processing channel. This increased cognitive load in the visual channel reduces the amount of processing that people can apply to the animation, which also enters through the visual channel. The top frame in Figure 9.3 shows that both pictures and printed words must enter the learner's information processing

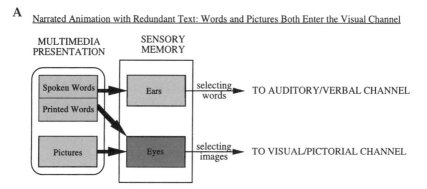

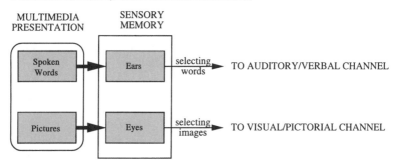

Figure 9.3   Why the cognitive theory of multimedia learning predicts that **(A)** animation with both narration and on-screen text is worse than **(B)** animation with narration only.

through the eyes and initially be represented as images in working memory (thus, both compete for resources within the visual channel); in contrast, the bottom frame in Figure 9.3 shows that pictures enter through the eyes (and are processed in the visual channel) whereas spoken words enter through the ears (and are processed in the verbal channel).

According to the cognitive theory of multimedia learning, meaningful learning occurs when people can attend to relevant portions of the incoming visual and auditory information, organize the material into coherent verbal and pictorial representations, and integrate the two representations. When pictures, printed words, and spoken words are all presented, the system can become overloaded in two ways. First, pictures and printed words compete for limited cognitive resources in the visual channel because both enter the information processing through the eyes. Second, when verbal information is presented both visually and auditorily, learners may be tempted to attend to both in an attempt to reconcile the two information streams; this extraneous activity requires cognitive resources that consequently are not available for processing the animation and mentally linking it with the narration, an integration process that is essential for meaningful learning. In contrast, the most efficient way to present verbal material is through the verbal channel – that is, as spoken text only – because in this way it does not compete with pictures for cognitive resources in the visual channel. On the basis of this theory, we can predict a *redundancy effect* in which adding on-screen text to a concise narrated animation will result in poorer learning, as indicated by the results of retention tests, and in poorer understanding, as indicated by the results of transfer tests.

Understanding the Redundancy Effect

Kalyuga, Chandler, and Sweller (1998, p. 2) have used the term *redundancy effect* in a broad sense to refer to any multimedia situation in which "eliminating redundant material results in better performance than when the redundant material is included." For example, in some situations, student learning is hurt when text is added to a multimedia instructional presentation, presumably because the text is redundant with the same information that has already been presented via diagrams or other sources (Bobis, Sweller, & Cooper, 1993; Chandler & Sweller, 1991; Kalyuga et al., 1998; Sweller & Chandler, 1994). In contrast, in this book I use the term *redundancy effect* in a more restricted sense to refer to any multimedia situation in which learning from animation (or illustrations) and narration is superior to learning from the same materials along with printed text that matches the narration.

The learning-preferences hypothesis and the limited-capacity hypothesis differ in their views about redundancy and in their conceptions of learning. First, the learning preferences hypothesis is based on the commonsense notion that presenting words in two ways (i.e., spoken and printed) is better than presenting words only in one way (i.e., spoken only). Tindall-Ford, Chandler, and Sweller (1997, p. 257) summarize this conventional view as follows: "Two sensory modalities are better than one." In contrast, the limited-capacity hypothesis holds that in some situations presenting words in one sense modality (i.e., spoken words) is better than presenting words in two modalities (i.e., as spoken words and printed words). In short, redundancy is not necessarily a virtue when it comes to the design of multimedia explanations.

Second, the learning-preferences hypothesis is based on the information-delivery theory of multimedia learning, in which the instructor's job is to present information and the student's job is to receive it. Each presentation format is a delivery system for information, so having two deliveries of the same words is better than having only one delivery. If one delivery is blocked – perhaps because the learner does not learn well from that format – then the information still gets through via another route. In contrast, the capacity-limitation hypothesis is based on the cognitive theory of multimedia learning, in which the learner actively builds a mental representation that makes sense to the learner. The process of knowledge construction requires that the learner select, organize, and integrate relevant visual and verbal information subject to limitations in visual and auditory processing. Presentation modes that overload a channel, such as presenting animation and words through the visual channel, hinder the process of knowledge construction.

RESEARCH ON REDUNDANCY

Does adding on-screen text to narrated animations affect student learning? To answer this question, we conducted a set of two studies in which we compared the retention and transfer performance of students who received one of two types of multimedia explanations: a narrated animation explaining how lightning storms develop or the same narrated animation along with concurrent on-screen text (Mayer, Heiser, & Lonn, in press, Experiments 1 and 2). The top panel of Figure 9.1 exemplifies the narrated animation treatment, whereas the bottom panel of Figure 9.1 exemplifies the narrated animation with on-screen text treatment. The retention test involved writing down an explanation for how lightning storms develop and was scored by tallying the number of essential steps that were recalled. The transfer test involved writing answers to such essay questions as "What could be done to reduce the intensity of a lightning storm?" and was scored by tallying the number of acceptable answers. According to the learning-preferences hypothesis, the narration-animation-text students should outperform the narration-animation students on tests of retention and transfer, but the capacity-limitation hypothesis makes the opposite prediction.

Redundancy Effect for Retention

Figure 9.4 shows the mean retention scores for students who received the narration-animation treatment and for those who received the narration-animation-text treatment. In both cases, narration-animation students remembered more of the steps in the process of lightning formation than did narration-animation-text students. We refer to this pattern as a *redundancy effect for retention* because adding on-screen text that is identical to the narration tends to hurt student learning. The redundancy effect for retention is that students perform more poorly on verbal retention when they learn with animation, narration, and text than when they learn with just animation and narration. The effect sizes for this redundancy effect, summarized in Figure 9.5, are consistent and moderately strong, with a median of .77. The percentage improvement in retention performance for the narration-animation students over the narration-animation-text students is also consistent

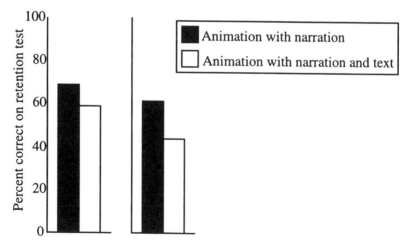

Figure 9.4 Redundancy effect for retention: better retention when words are presented as narration (*dark bars*) rather than as narration and on-screen text (*white bars*).

Figure 9.5 Redundancy Effect for Retention: Summary of Results

Source	Content	Effect size	Percent gain
Mayer et al., in press, Exp. 1	Lightning	.66	16
Mayer et al., in press, Exp. 2	Lightning	.88	41
Median		**.77**	**28**

and moderately strong, with a mean of 28%; that is, the narration-animation students remembered 28% more of the important material than did the narration-animation-text students.

Redundancy Effect for Transfer

Figure 9.6 shows the mean transfer scores for students who received the narration-animation treatment and for those who received the narration-animation-text treatment. In both cases, narration-animation students generated more solutions to problems about lightning formation than did narration-animation-text students. We refer to this pattern as a *redundancy effect for transfer* because adding on-screen text that is identical to the narration tends to hurt student understanding. In short, the redundancy effect for transfer is that students perform more poorly on problem-solving transfer when they learn with animation, narration, and text than when they learn with animation and narration. The redundancy effect sizes, summarized in Figure 9.7, are consistent

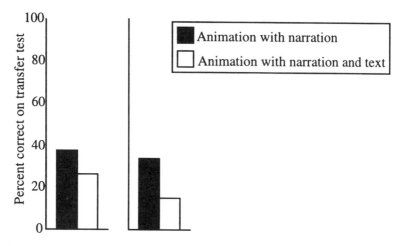

Figure 9.6 Redundancy effect for transfer: better transfer when words are presented as narration (*dark bars*) rather than as narration and on-screen text (*white bars*).

Figure 9.7   Redundancy Effect for Transfer: Summary of Results

Source	Content	Effect size	Percent gain
Mayer et al., in press, Exp. 1	Lightning	.84	42
Mayer et al., in press, Exp. 2	Lightning	1.65	117
Median		**1.24**	**79**

and strong, with a median of 1.24. In addition, the percentage gain on transfer for the narration-animation students over that for the narration-animation-text group is consistent and strong, with a median of 79%; that is, the narration-animation students generated 79% more creative solutions on the transfer test than did the narration-animation-text students.

Overall, the redundancy effect is consistent with the cognitive theory of multimedia learning (and its capacity-limitation hypothesis) and inconsistent with the information delivery theory of multimedia learning (and its learning-preferences hypothesis).

Related Research

Redundancy effects have also been obtained using static diagrams, speech, and printed text (Kalyuga, Chandler, & Sweller, 1999). For example, Kalyuga, Chandler, and Sweller (1999) trained people in how to solder metals in an industrial setting. Some people learned by using diagrams with accompanying printed text, some people learned with diagrams and accompanying speech (which contained the same words as the text), and some learned with diagrams accompanied by both text and speech. The results revealed a redundancy effect in which people who learned from diagrams and speech performed better on subsequent soldering tasks than did people receiving diagrams along with both speech and text. Our results complement and extend this finding in two ways: (1) by demonstrating that redundancy effects occur in multimedia environments involving animation, on-screen text, and narration, and (2) by using a rich set of dependent measures that assess both retention and transfer.

IMPLICATIONS

Implications for Multimedia Learning

In two separate tests, learning a scientific explanation from a concise narrated animation was hurt by the addition of on-screen text that contained the same words as the narration. We refer to this finding as a *redundancy effect*: Adding redundant on-screen text to a narrated animation detracts from multimedia learning.

The redundancy effect provides important support for the cognitive theory of multimedia learning and its capacity-limitation hypothesis. In particular, the redundancy effect is consistent with the capacity-limitation hypothesis, in which visual working memory becomes overloaded when animation and on-screen text are presented concurrently (as in the narration-animation-text treatment). In this case, fewer cognitive resources are available for making connections between corresponding words and pictures, thus decreasing the chances for meaningful learning. In contrast, when words are presented in the auditory channel and pictures are presented in the visual channel (as in the narration-animation treatment), the load on these systems is minimized. In this case, more cognitive resources are available for making connections between corresponding words and pictures, so the chances for meaningful learning are increased.

The redundancy effect is not consistent with the learning-preferences hypothesis, in which adding redundant on-screen text to a narrated animation is supposed to allow learners to choose the mode of presentation for words – visual or auditory – that best fits their learning style. The learning-preferences hypothesis predicts that redundancy will enhance student learning, but our results were the opposite. We caution, however, that the redundancy effect does not invalidate the value of allowing learners some choice in adjusting multimedia presentations to fit their learning preferences in some situations. For example, Plass, Chun, Mayer, and Leutner (1998) found that allowing students to choose between pictorial and verbal definitions of words helped them learn the words while reading a story in a second-language-learning multimedia environment.

What is the relation between the redundancy principle and the multimedia principle (as described in chapter 4)? The redundancy principle seems to suggest that two modalities are worse than one, whereas the multimedia principle seems to suggest that two modalities are better than one. The apparent discrepancy can be resolved by applying the cognitive theory of multimedia learning. The redundancy principle is based on a situation in which presenting words in two sense modalities – as print and as speech – is worse than presenting words solely in one modality – as speech. A distinguishing feature in this situation is that the added on-screen text serves to overload the visual channel, which must also process the incoming animation. In contrast, the multimedia principle is based on the idea that learning can be improved when a narration is supplemented with corresponding animation. In this case, load on the visual channel is not increased because words are presented in the auditory channel.

What is the relation between the redundancy principle and the modality principle (as described in chapter 8)? According to the cognitive theory of multimedia learning, not all techniques for removing redundancy are equally effective. For example, when a multimedia explanation is presented using animation, narration, and text, one effective way to remove redundancy is to remove the on-screen text, yielding the redundancy effect described in this chapter. However, an alternative method of removing redundancy is to remove the narration. According to the cognitive theory of multimedia learning, this situation can overload the visual channel because words and pictures are both presented visually. In chapter 8, we use the term *modality effect* to refer to the situation in which learning from animation with narration is more effective than learning from animation with on-screen text. In both cases – the redundancy effect and the modality effect – learning is more efficient when words are presented in spoken form and not in printed form; however, in the redundancy effect, learning is hurt by starting with a concise narrated animation and adding on-screen text, whereas in the modality effect, learning is hurt by starting with a CNA and substituting on-screen text for narration.

Implications for Multimedia Design

The redundancy effect allows us to add another principle of multimedia design to our collection: When making a multimedia presentation consisting of a concise narrated animation, do not add on-screen text that duplicates words that are already in the narration. This design principle has been demonstrated in situations in which the animated narration runs at a fast rate without learner control of the presentation.

The redundancy effect should not be taken as justification for never presenting printed and spoken text together. In my opinion, multimedia design principles should not be applied as unbending commandments but rather should be interpreted in light of theories of how people learn, such as the cognitive theory of multimedia learning. Presenting words in spoken and printed form may be harmful in some situations – such as in the studies described in this chapter – but not in other situations – such as when the rate of presentation is slow or when no pictorial material is concurrently presented. For example, it might be useful to present summary slides (or to write key ideas on a chalkboard) in the course of a verbal presentation or lecture. This is a research question that warrants further study. In contrast, the research reviewed in this chapter suggests that it is harmful to present printed and spoken text together when pictorial information is also presented visually and when the material is presented at a rapid pace without opportunity for learner control of the presentation.

This chapter began with the question "How can we improve concise narrated animations?" The answer is that adding redundant on-screen text is not an effective way to improve on a concise narrated animation. On the basis of the research reviewed in this chapter, it appears that the best approach to redesigning a concise narrated animation is to simply leave it as is.

SUGGESTED READINGS

Kalyuga, S., Chandler, P. & Sweller, P. (1999). Managing split-attention and redundancy in multimedia instruction. *Applied Cognitive Psychology, 13,* 351–372.

*Mayer, R. E., Heiser, J., & Lonn, S. (in press). Cognitive constraints on multimedia learning: When presenting more material results in less understanding. *Journal of Educational Psychology.*

---

* Asterisk indicates that part of the chapter is based on this publication.

10

Individual Differences Principle

Individual Differences Principle: Design effects are stronger for low-knowledge learners than for high-knowledge learners, and for high-spatial learners rather than for low-spatial learners.

Theoretical Rationale: High-knowledge learners are able to use their prior knowledge to compensate for lack of guidance in the presentation – such as by forming appropriate mental images from words – whereas low-knowledge learners are less able to engage in useful cognitive processing when the presentation lacks guidance. High-spatial learners possess the cognitive capacity to mentally integrate visual and verbal representations from effective multimedia presentations; in contrast, low-spatial learners must devote so much cognitive capacity to holding the presented images in memory that they are less likely to have sufficient capacity left over to mentally integrate visual and verbal representations.

Empirical Rationale: In two of three tests, low-knowledge learners achieved higher gains on retention tests from implementing multimedia design principles than did high-knowledge learners. In four of four tests, low-knowledge learners achieved higher gains on transfer tests from implementing multimedia design principles than did high-knowledge learners. In two of two tests, high-spatial learners achieved greater gains on transfer tests from implementing multimedia design principles than did low-spatial learners. There were not tests involving retention tests for high- and low-spatial learners.

■■ Chapter Outline

QUESTIONS ABOUT MULTIMEDIA LEARNING

The first three chapters in this book examined the nature of multimedia learning – answering the question "What is multimedia learning?" – and described a cognitive theory of multimedia learning, aimed at addressing the question "Why does multimedia learning work?" Then, in chapter 4, I reviewed research aimed at addressing the question "Does multimedia work?" In answer to this question, research on the multimedia principle demonstrated that in some cases, students learn more deeply when instructional messages are presented in words and pictures rather than in words alone. Not all multimedia presentations are equally effective, so the next step in our research review was to examine the conditions under which multimedia works.

In chapters 5 through 9, the research review shifted to the question "When does multimedia work?" In answering this question, I explored five conditions under which multimedia presentations may lead to deeper learning, as reflected in the spatial-contiguity, temporal-contiguity, coherence, modality, and redundancy principles. These principles allow us to design high-quality multimedia presentations but lead to the issue of whether they are equally effective for all learners.

In this chapter, I explore the question "For whom does multimedia work?" Another way to ask this question is: "Are there important individual differences in which applying the principles of multimedia design tends to help some kinds of learners more than others?" In this chapter, I address the issue of who benefits most from high-quality multimedia presentations. In particular, I focus on two kinds of individual differences: Differences in learners' existing knowledge – which form the basis for individual differences principle 1 – and differences in learners' spatial ability – which form the basis for individual differences principle 2.

INDIVIDUAL DIFFERENCES PRINCIPLE 1: ROLE OF LEARNER'S EXISTING KNOWLEDGE

Introduction

Who Benefits from Well-Designed Multimedia Presentations?

On the basis of the principles that have emerged in the foregoing chapters, it is possible to produce a well-designed multimedia message. In the case of a book-based presentation such as in Figure 2.1, the message is *contiguous* (i.e., corresponding words and pictures are near each other) and *coherent* (i.e., extra words and pictures are excluded). In short, it consists of annotated illustrations that are coordinated and concise. In the case of a computer-based presentation such as in Figure 2.2, the message is *contiguous* (i.e., corresponding words and pictures are presented simultaneously), *coherent* (i.e., extra words and pictures are excluded), *modality efficient* (i.e., words are not presented as narration), and *nonredundant* (i.e., words are not presented as on-screen text that duplicates the narration). In short, it consists of a narrated animation that is coordinated and concise.

In chapters 4 through 9, we have seen that applying these basic design principles generally results in students' remembering more of the conceptually important information and being able to generate more solutions to problems. My goal in this chapter is to determine whether improving the design of multimedia messages benefits some kinds of learners more than others. In this section, I focus on the role of the learner's existing knowledge, and in particular, I focus on the learner's knowledge about the domain of the lesson.

For example, please complete the questionnaire in Figure 10.1. For the top part, place a check mark next to each item that applies to you; for the bottom part, place a check mark indicating your knowledge of meteorology.

Figure 10.1   Meteorology Questionnaire

Please place a check mark next to the items that apply to you:

_____   I regularly read the weather maps in a newspaper.
_____   I know what a cold front is.
_____   I can distinguish between cumulous and nimbus clouds.
_____   I know what low pressure is.
_____   I can explain what makes wind blow.
_____   I know what this symbol means: 
_____   I know what this symbol means:

Please put a check mark indicating your knowledge of meteorology (weather):
_____   Very much

_____   Average

_____   Very little

The purpose of this little questionnaire is to obtain a quick and simple assessment of your knowledge of meteorology. To score the questionnaire, give yourself 1 point for each item you checked in the list at the top of the figure and add 1 to 5 more points on the basis of your level of knowledge (1 point for "very little" and up to 5 points for "very much"). If your total score was 6 or less, you would be considered a low-knowledge learner in our research on the lightning lesson; if your total score was 7 or more, you would be considered a high-knowledge learner with respect to the lightning lesson.

Figure 10.2   Car Mechanics Questionnaire

Please place a check mark next to the things you have done:

_____   I have obtained a driver's license.
_____   I have put air into a car's tire.
_____   I have changed a tire on a car.
_____   I have changed the oil in a car.
_____   I have installed spark plugs in a car.
_____   I have replaced the brake shoes in a car.

Please place a check mark indicating your knowledge of car mechanics and repair:

_____   Very much

_____   Average

_____   Very little

Figure 10.3 Household Repair Questionnaire

Please place a check mark next to the things you have done:

_____ I own a screwdriver.
_____ I own a power saw.
_____ I have replaced the heads on a lawn sprinkler system.
_____ I have replaced the washer in a sink faucet.
_____ I have replaced the flush mechanism in a toilet.
_____ I have replaced or installed plumbing pipes or fixtures.

Please place a check mark indicating your knowledge of how to fix household appliances and machines:

_____ Very much

_____ Average

_____ Very little

Figure 10.2 presents a similar knowledge questionnaire that we used to assess students' knowledge of car mechanics (for use with the brakes lesson) and Figure 10.3 presents a questionnaire that we used to assess knowledge of household repair (for use with the pump lesson). These questionnaires were scored similarly to the meteorology questionnaire. As you can see, our goal is to obtain a rough measurement of how much knowledge a person has about a specific topic – such as weather (in Figure 10.1) for the lightning lesson, car mechanics (in Figure 10.2) for the brakes lesson, and household repair (Figure 10.3) for the pump lesson. Thus, when I talk about the learner's existing knowledge, I mean the learner's knowledge and familiarity with specific situations that are related to the lesson's theme. This can be called *domain-specific knowledge* because it is knowledge about a specific set of situations.

The role of prior knowledge – that is, the domain-specific knowledge that a learner brings to the learning task – has a long and important history in research on learning, particularly learning from text (Bransford, Brown, & Cocking, 1999; Lambert & McCombs, 1998; Mayer, 1999c). Research on reading comprehension shows that what students learn from reading a passage depends both on the information contained in the passage and the reader's existing knowledge. High-knowledge readers tend to remember more material from a passage they have read than do low-knowledge readers; in particular, the recall protocols of high-knowledge readers contain more high-level conceptual material and more inferences than do the recall protocols of low-knowledge readers. In addition, students who bring different kinds of knowledge to a reading comprehension task may come away with different learning outcomes. In particular, students tend to remember material that is related to their existing knowledge and to not remember material that is unrelated to their existing knowledge.

What is the role of the learner's existing knowledge in multimedia learning? In particular, do some learners benefit more than others from implementing the good design principles described in this book? In this section, I examine three possible answers: knowledge doesn't matter, knowledge compensates for poor design, knowledge enhances good design.

The Case for Not Considering Learner Knowledge

According to the information-delivery theory, none of the principles I have described so far in this book should be effective. Therefore, it makes no sense to try to determine for whom they are most effective. Implementing the principles should be equally ineffective for both low- and high-knowledge learners. The premise underlying this approach is that learner knowledge doesn't matter when implementing design principles.

This approach does not mean that individual differences are not related to overall levels of learning. According to the information-delivery theory, if a learner has a particularly effective delivery system – for example, if high knowledge effectively increases the amount of information that can be delivered – then that learner will acquire more information than will a learner who has a particularly ineffective delivery system. In this way, knowledge can influence the overall amount learned but should not have different effects depending on the whether the instructional message was based on good design principles. This pattern is depicted in the left panel of Figure 10-4: High-knowledge learners outperform low-knowledge learners (as is indicated by one line being higher than the other), but good and poor instruction produce the same effects (as is indicated by each line being flat).

The Case for Targeting Low-Knowledge Learners

In contrast, the cognitive theory of multimedia learning is based on the idea that learner understanding depends on being able to make connections between corresponding visual and verbal representations held in working memory at the same time. When poorly designed instruction is presented, high-knowledge learners may be able to use their knowledge to compensate, but low-knowledge learners cannot. When well-designed instruction is presented, high- and low-knowledge learners will both be able to understand the presentation. In this scenario, low-knowledge learners would benefit most from implementing design principles – that is, they would show a larger improve-

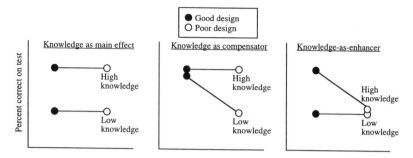

Figure 10.4 Three views of the interaction of knowledge and design.

ment in moving from poorly designed to well-designed messages than would high-knowledge learners. This approach to the cognitive theory of multimedia learning is based on the idea that high-knowledge compensates for poor instruction.

The middle panel of Figure 10.4 depicts this knowledge-as-compensator situation: For high-knowledge learners, the line is high and flat, indicating high performance for both poor and good instruction, whereas for low-knowledge learners, the line is sloped, showing low performance for poor instruction and high performance for good instruction.

The Case for Targeting High-Knowledge Learners

An alternative approach to the cognitive theory of multimedia learning is based on the idea that high knowledge enhances good instruction. Consistent with the cognitive theory of multimedia learning, learner understanding depends on being able to make connections between corresponding visual and verbal representations held in working memory at the same time. When poorly designed instruction is presented, both low- and high-knowledge learners suffer because the message does not present corresponding visual and verbal material in a concise and coordinated way. When well-designed instruction is presented, high-knowledge learners can take advantage of and use the material to build coherent mental representations, whereas low-knowledge learners must struggle so much with processing the basic material that they have no cognitive resources left for deeper processing. In this scenario, high-knowledge learners would benefit most from implementing design principles; that is, they would show a larger improvement in moving from poorly designed to well-designed messages than would low-knowledge learners.

The third panel in Figure 10.4 depicts this knowledge-as-enhancer view: The line is low and flat for low-knowledge learners (indicating low performance with both kinds of instruction), whereas the line is sloped for high-knowledge learners (indicating low performance for poor instruction and high performance for good instruction).

Research on Individual Differences in Knowledge

Does changing a poorly designed instructional message into a well-designed one have different consequences depending on the learner's existing knowledge? In particular does the level of the learner's existing knowledge have the same effect for good and poor instruction, act as a compensator for poor instruction, or act as a enhancer for good instruction? To provide some preliminary data on these questions, my colleagues and I conducted four separate comparisons in which we compared the test performance of high- and low-knowledge students who learned from well-designed and poorly designed instructional messages (Mayer, Steinhoff, Bower, & Mars, 1995, Experiment 2; Mayer & Gallini, 1990, Experiments 1 through 3). All the comparisons involved a book-based environment. In three of the comparisons, the poorly designed message consisted of text alone, whereas the well-designed message consisted of both text and illustrations to allow testing for a multimedia effect (Mayer & Gallini, 1990, Experiments 1 through 3); in one of the comparisons, the poorly designed message presented text and illustrations that were separated, whereas the well-designed message presented text and illustrations that were integrated to allow testing for a spatial-contiguity effect (Mayer, Steinhoff, et al., 1995, Experiment 2).

Our main focus is on whether the multimedia effect or spatial contiguity was different for low-knowledge versus high-knowledge learners. According to the information-delivery theory, the multimedia effect and spatial-contiguity effect should be the same for low- and for high-knowledge learners. In contrast, the knowledge-as-compensation version of the cognitive theory of multimedia learning predicts that low-knowledge learners will show greater multimedia and spatial-contiguity effects than will high-knowledge learners.

Knowledge Effect for Retention

Figure 10.5 summarizes the percent correct answers given on the retention test by low-knowledge learners who received text only, by low-knowledge learners who received text and illustrations, by high-knowledge learners who received text only, and by high-knowledge learners who received text and illustrations. A multimedia effect would be reflected in better retention test performance for presentations con-

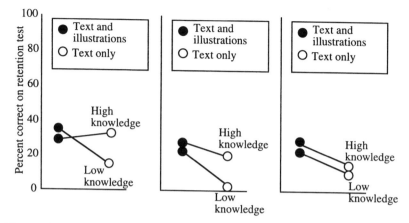

Figure 10.5 Knowledge effect for retention: strong design effects for low-knowledge but not for high-knowledge learners.

taining multiple representations (i.e., text and illustrations) than for presentations containing a single representation (i.e., text alone). As you can see in each of the three cases presented in Figure 10.5, there is a strong multimedia effect for low-knowledge learners but not for high-knowledge learners.

For each of the three comparisons, I computed an effect size difference by subtracting the effect size for the high-knowledge learners from the effect size for the low-knowledge learners, and I computed a percent gain difference by subtracting the percent gain for the high-knowledge learners from the percent gain for the low-knowledge learners. Figure 10.6 presents the effect size difference and the percent gain difference for each of the three tests involving retention. As you can see, the difference in effect size varies from study to study, with a median of .60; in short, the multimedia effect was .60 standard deviations stronger for low-knowledge learners than for high-knowledge learners. Similarly, the difference in percent gain varies from study to study, with a median of 157%; in short, the multimedia effect was 157

Figure 10.6 Knowledge Effect for Retention: Summary of Results

Source	Content	Context	Effect size difference	Percent gain difference
Mayer and Gallini, 1990, Exp. 1	Brakes	Page	1.60	157
Mayer and Gallini, 1990, Exp. 2	Pumps	Page	.60	582
Mayer and Gallini, 1990, Exp. 3	Generator	Page	.00	00
Median			**.60**	**157**

percentage points stronger for low- than for high-knowledge learners. On average, these median scores show that low-knowledge learners benefited more from improving the design of the instructional messages than did high-knowledge learners.

Knowledge Effect for Transfer

For each of four comparisons, Figure 10.7 summarizes the percent correct on the transfer test for low- and for high-knowledge learners who received well-designed instructional messages and for those of both kinds of learners who received poorly designed instructional messages. In three of the studies, the well-designed message included text and illustrations, whereas the poorly designed message contained text only. In these studies, a multimedia effect would be reflected in better transfer test performance for presentations containing multiple representations (i.e., words and pictures) than for presentations containing a single representation (i.e., words alone). In one of the studies, the well-designed message included text that was integrated with illustrations and the poorly designed message had text that was separated from illustrations. In this study, a spatial-contiguity effect would be reflected in better transfer performance for integrated rather than for separated presentations. As you can see in each of the four cases presented in Figure 10.7, there is a strong multimedia or spatial-contiguity effect for low-knowledge learners but not for high-knowledge learners.

As with the retention test results, I computed an effect size difference for the transfer results by subtracting the effect size for the high-knowledge learners from the effect size for the low-knowledge learners, and I computed a percent gain difference for the transfer results by subtracting the percent gain for the high-knowledge learners from the

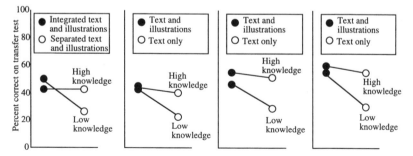

Figure 10.7   Knowledge effect for transfer: strong effects for low-knowledge but not for high-knowledge learners.

Figure 10.8 Knowledge Effect for Transfer: Summary of Results

Source	Content	Context	Effect size difference	Percent gain difference
Mayer, Steinhoff, et al., 1995, Exp. 2	Lightning	Page	1.35	89
Mayer and Gallini, 1990, Exp. 1	Brakes	Page	.82	64
Mayer and Gallini, 1990, Exp. 2	Pumps	Page	.79	59
Mayer and Gallini, 1990, Exp. 3	Generator	Page	1.09	82
Median			**.80**	**61**

percent gain for the low-knowledge learners. Figure 10.8 presents the effect size difference and the percent gain difference for each of the four tests involving transfer. As you can see, the difference in effect size is consistent and moderately strong, with a median of .80; similarly, the difference in percent gain is consistent and moderately strong, with a median of 61 percentage points. On average, these median scores show that low-knowledge learners benefited more from improving the design of the multimedia messages than did high-knowledge learners.

Overall, the results do not support the prediction of the information-delivery theory that implementing design principles would have the same effect on both low- and high-knowledge learners. In contrast, the results are consistent with a version of the cognitive theory of multimedia learning in which domain knowledge compensates for poor instruction. However, more research is needed using different kinds of principles and instructional materials.

Related Research

There is converging evidence that high-quality multimedia design is more important for low- rather than high-experience learners. In one set of studies (Kalyuga, Chandler, & Sweller, 1998), learners with low levels and those with high levels of expertise learned about the operation of a bell-and-light circuit. Low-expertise learners learned better when diagrams and text were physically integrated than when they were separated or when only the diagram was presented; however, the reverse pattern was produced for high-expertise learners, who learned best from the diagram alone. In another set of studies (Kalyuga, Chandler, & Sweller, 2000), both low- and high-experience workers learned to operate a drilling machine on the basis of a diagram with auditory narration or a diagram alone. Low-experience learners performed best with the diagram and narration, whereas high-experience learners performed best with the diagram alone. It appears that integrating words and pictures is most helpful for learners who lack much experience in a domain.

INDIVIDUAL DIFFERENCES PRINCIPLE 2: ROLE OF LEARNER'S SPATIAL ABILITY

Introduction

Who Benefits from Well-Designed Multimedia Presentations?

The foregoing section shows that the benefits of applying cognitively based principles to the design of multimedia messages may depend on the level of knowledge that the learner brings to the learning situation. In particular, the foregoing section shows how low-knowledge learners benefit more from incorporating design principles into multimedia presentations than do high-knowledge learners. This line of research shows that multimedia designers need to consider the learner's prior knowledge. In this section, I continue the search for individual differences that might be important in multimedia learning. In particular, I focus on the role of spatial ability.

Spatial ability is generally defined as the ability to generate, maintain, and manipulate mental visual images (Carroll, 1993). For example, when reading a sentence that says "A stepped leader of negative charges moves downward in steps," a person may be able to form a mental image of a zigzag downward path. This is an example of generating a mental image. Later, when reading "A positively charged leader travels up from such objects as trees and buildings," the person may need to generate an image of an upward-moving leader and also keep in mind the image of the downward-moving one. Remembering the image of the downward-moving leader is an example of maintaining a mental image. The reader may also be able to mentally visualize that the downward and upward leaders will meet. This is an example of manipulating a mental image.

Why focus on spatial ability? Our rationale is that the ability to engage in spatial cognition is particularly important in multimedia learning. Conventional instructional messages are heavily verbal, but multimedia messages are verbal *and* visual – so multimedia learners need to be able to form, hold, and use mental images. Thus, some of the skills that are required to engage fully in multimedia learning seem to closely resemble the definition of spatial ability.

How can we measure spatial ability? Although there are hundreds of spatial-ability tests, we selected short versions of two classic tests of spatial ability – a ten-item paper-folding test intended to evaluate a component of spatial ability called visualization and an eighty-item mental rotation test intended to evaluate a component of spatial ability called spatial relations. Each test had a three-minute time limit and was taken from a battery of cognitive tests developed by Ekstrom, French, and Harman (1976).

Consider the paper-folding test item shown in Figure 10.9A. In this test, you should assume that we fold a sheet paper one or more times, then punch one or more holes in it, and then unfold the paper back into its original form. Your job is to select, from a set of five possible answers, the alternative that corresponds to how the sheet will look. Go ahead and circle one of the five alternatives for the item at the top of Figure 10.9. If you selected the third alternative, you were correct. However, I must warn you that some of the items on the test can get a bit more complicated – by folding the paper more times and punching more holes.

In our research we used a ten-item test of paper folding in which the problems increase in complexity; that is, later problems involve more folds and more holes than earlier ones. First, students read instructions and saw a sample problem similar to the one in the top of Figure 10.9, and then they had three minutes to solve ten paper-folding problems. We scored the test by counting the number of correct answers, with a range of possible correct answers of 0 to 10.

Next, consider the row of mental rotation test items shown in the bottom of Figure 10.9. Look at the figure on the left; this is the standard. Then, for each item on the right place a check mark in the S box if the item is the same as the standard and place a check mark in the D box if it is different from the standard. It is the same if you could rotate the figure clockwise or counterclockwise to get it to look exactly like the standard. It is different if you would have to flip it over to get it to look exactly like the standard. Go ahead and place check marks in the S or D box for each of the eight items. The correct answers are: SDSSDDDS.

In our research, we used an eighty-item test of mental rotation in which each row of eight problems was based on the same standard, but a different standard was given in each row. First, students read instructions and saw practice problems similar to those shown in Figure 10.9B, and then they had three minutes to solve the eighty mental rotations problems. We scored the test by counting the number of correct answers and dividing the total by 8, yielding a possible range of 0 to 10. Then we added the score for the paper folding test to the score for the mental rotation test to generate a combined spatial-ability score, with a possible range of 0 to 20. We classified students who scored above the

174

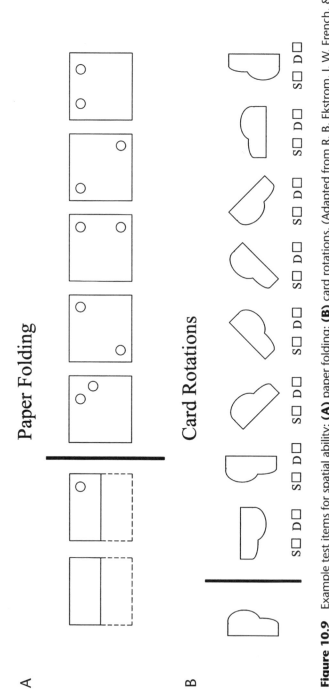

Figure 10.9 Example test items for spatial ability: **(A)** paper folding; **(B)** card rotations. (Adapted from R. B. Ekstrom, J. W. French, & H. H. Harman (1976): *Manual for kit of factor-referenced cognitive tests,* Princeton, NJ: Educational Testing Service. Educational Testing Service retains copyright in all kit test materials. (Adapted by permission of Educational Testing Service, the copyright holder.)

median as high-spatial ability learners, and those who scored below the median were classified as low-spatial ability learners. This gives us a very rough way to categorize learners based on two short tests of spatial ability.

Does improving the design of multimedia presentations have different effects on low- and high-spatial ability students? Let's consider three possibilities: (1) using well-designed multimedia presentations might have the same effect on both low- and high-spatial learners; (2) low-spatial learners might benefit most from well-designed multimedia presentations; or (3) high-spatial learners might benefit most from well-designed multimedia presentations. I examine each of these possibilities in turn in the next three sections.

The Case for Not Considering Spatial Ability

According to the information-delivery theory, implementing the design principles I have described in chapters 5 through 9 should not result in improved learning. Further, implementing the design principles should be equally ineffective for low- and for high-spatial learners. Thus, the information-delivery theory predicts that changing from poorly designed to well-designed multimedia presentations should have the same effects on both low- and high-spatial learners; that is, it should have no strong effect for either type of learner.

This theory does not preclude the possibility that high-spatial learners perform better overall than do low-spatial learners. High-spatial learners may have a more effective system for receiving delivered information than do low-spatial learners. This pattern is the same as the one depicted in the left panel of Figure 10.4, except that "Low knowledge" and "High knowledge" should be changed to "Low spatial" and "High spatial," respectively.

The Case for Targeting Low-Spatial Learners

The case for targeting low-spatial learners is based on the compensation view, in which spatial ability compensates for poor instruction. For example, one form of poorly designed instruction is to violate the temporal contiguity principle by presenting words and corresponding pictures at different times. When presented with a narration segment, a student who has high-spatial ability might be able to form an appropriate verbal representation and an appropriate pictorial representation. Thus, presenting the words and pictures simultaneously would not improve learning, because high-spatial learners are able to build their own visual representations from the words alone. In contrast, a low-spatial learner would be less likely to build an appropriate visual representation from a narration segment. Instead, the low-spatial student needs to have the simultaneous presentations of corresponding animation and narration segments. According to this view, low-spatial students learn better when words and pictures are presented in a coordinated way rather than in an uncoordinated way, but high-spatial students learn well under both conditions. This approach is depicted in the middle panel of Figure 10.4, except that "Low knowledge" and "High knowledge" should be changed to "Low spatial" and "High spatial," respectively.

The Case for Targeting High-Spatial Learners

The case for targeting high-spatial learners is based on the enhancement view, in which high spatial ability enables students to take advantage of high-quality multimedia presentations. For example, when animation and narration are presented successively, both low- and high-spatial learners will perform poorly because of the difficulty in holding corresponding pictorial and verbal representations in working memory at the same time. When animation and narration are presented simultaneously, high-spatial learners are more able to build connections between corresponding pictorial and verbal representations in working memory as described in the cognitive theory of multimedia learning; in contrast, low-spatial learners must devote so much energy to holding the visual images that they are less likely to be able to build connections between verbal and pictorial representations. In this way, spatial ability serves to enhance well-designed instruction. This pattern is reflected in the third panel of Figure 10.4, except that "High knowledge" and "Low knowledge" should be changed to "High spatial" and "Low spatial," respectively.

Research on Individual Differences in Spatial Ability

Does changing a poorly designed instructional message into a well-designed one have different consequences depending on the learner's spatial ability? My colleagues and I have collected some preliminary results that help address this question. In two studies, we compared the transfer test performance of high- versus low-spatial students who learned from well-designed and from poorly designed instructional messages (Mayer & Sims, 1994, Experiments 1 and 2). All the comparisons involved a computer-based environment and included transfer but not retention tests. In the well-designed messages, we presented narration and animation simultaneously, whereas in the poorly designed messages, we presented the narration and animation successively. A temporal contiguity effect would be reflected in better test performance for simultaneous than for successive presentations, as described in chapter 6.

Our main focus is on whether the temporal-contiguity effect is different for low-spatial ability than for high-spatial ability learners. According to the information-delivery theory, the temporal-contiguity effect should be equally strong for low and high-spatial ability learners. In contrast, the spatial-ability-as-enhancer version of the cognitive theory of multimedia learning predicts that high-spatial ability learners will show a greater temporal contiguity effect than will low-spatial ability learners.

Spatial Ability Effect for Transfer

Figure 10.10 shows the temporal contiguity effects on transfer for low- and for high-spatial ability learners in two separate studies. In both cases, there is a pattern in which simultaneous presentation results in better transfer performance than does successive presentation for high-spatial ability learners but not for low-spatial ability learners. In short, there appears to be a temporal contiguity effect for high- but not for low-spatial ability learners. This pattern is an example of an *individual differences effect for transfer* because improving the design of a multimedia message affects transfer performance differently for different kinds of learners.

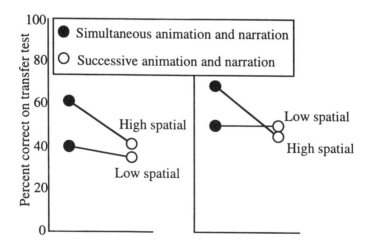

Figure 10.10   Spatial ability effect for transfer: strong design effects for high-spatial ability but not for low-spatial ability learners.

Figure 10.11 Spatial Ability Effect for Transfer: Summary of Results

Source	Content	Context	Effect size difference	Percent gain difference
Mayer and Sims, 1994, Exp. 1	Brakes	Screen	.66	36
Mayer and Sims, 1994, Exp. 2	Lungs	Screen	1.60	56
Median			**1.13**	**46**

Figure 10.11 shows that the effect size difference for transfer in each the two studies is moderate to strong, with a median of 1.13. Another way to summarize this result is to say that the temporal contiguity effect is more than 1 standard deviation greater for high-spatial ability learners than for low-spatial ability learners. Figure 10.11 also shows that the percent gain difference for transfer in each of the two studies is moderate, with a median of 46 percentage points. In short, the percent gain of the simultaneous over the successive group was an average of 46 percentage points higher for high-spatial ability learners than for low-spatial ability learners. Overall, the results provide consistent preliminary evidence that high-spatial ability learners benefit more from improved multimedia design than do low-spatial ability learners.

This pattern of results is inconsistent with the information-delivery theory and its prediction that implementing design principles would have the same effect on both low- and high-spatial learners. The pattern of results is consistent with a version of the cognitive theory of multimedia learning in which spatial ability is seen as an enhancer of well-designed instruction. However, given the low number of comparisons, more research is needed.

Related Research

Although spatial ability may be an important factor in multimedia learning, it has not yet been widely studied. For example, Leutner and Plass (1998) developed a computer-based method for assessing visualizer/verbalizer learning preferences – that is, the degree to which multimedia students prefer to use visualizer versus verbalizer learning strategies. Plass, Chun, Mayer, & Leutner (1998) were able to detect differences in the effectiveness of various multimedia design features based on the visual and verbal preferences of the learners. One important conclusion is that learners need to be able to choose whether instructional material will be presented in words or pictures. Additional research is needed to pinpoint the role of spatial ability in multimedia learning.

IMPLICATIONS

Implications for Multimedia Learning

The characteristics that a learner brings to the learning situation influence the effectiveness of implementing multimedia design principles. In four separate tests, low-knowledge learners benefited more from improvements in the design of a multimedia message than did high-knowledge learners. In two separate tests, high-spatial learners benefited more from improvements in the design of a multimedia message than did low-spatial learners. I refer to these findings as an *individual differences effect*: Design effects are stronger for low- rather than for high-knowledge learners and for high- rather than low-spatial learners.

The individual differences effect involving knowledge is consistent with the cognitive theory of multimedia learning. For example, consider the case of poorly designed multimedia messages in which the words are not presented with corresponding pictures. The individual differences effect involving knowledge is consistent with the idea that high-knowledge learners are more likely to be able to construct pictorial and verbal representations from words alone and thus are more likely to have corresponding pictorial and verbal representations in their working memories at the same time. In short, they can use their domain knowledge to help build a pictorial representation based on verbal input. In contrast, low-knowledge learners are less likely to be able to construct a pictorial representation from words alone and therefore are less likely to have corresponding pictorial and verbal representations in working memory at the same time. When well-designed messages are presented, both high- and low-knowledge learners are expected to learn well because both are able to construct pictorial and verbal representations and hold them in working memory at the same time. According to this analysis, high-knowledge learners will learn more deeply from a poorly designed instructional message than will low-knowledge learners because high-knowledge learners are better able to construct both pictorial and verbal mental representations when only words are presented.

The individual differences effect involving spatial ability is also consistent with the cognitive theory of multimedia learning. Again, consider what happens when a poorly designed message is presented. In this case, both low- and high-spatial learners will have difficulty in constructing visual and verbal representations that are held in working memory at the same time. A high level of spatial ability may not be sufficient to construct a visual representation from words alone, especially when the verbal description is based on specific domain knowledge (such as knowing what a piston looks like). Accordingly, the cognitive theory of multimedia learning predicts that both low- and high-spatial learners will perform at similar levels for poorly designed instructional messages. However, when a well-designed message is presented, high-spatial learners can construct corresponding visual and verbal representations and make appropriate connections between them. In contrast, low-spatial learners may need to expend so much energy in constructing and holding visual representations that they do not have much capacity left for building connections between the visual and verbal representations. Accordingly, high-spatial learners are more likely to benefit from well-designed messages than are low-spatial learners.

The individual differences effect is not consistent with the information-delivery theory. In its most stark form, the information-delivery theory predicts that individual differences affect all presentations the same way. Implementing design principles should have the same effects on both low- and high-knowledge learners and on both low- and high-spatial ability learners. As we have seen in previous chapters, the information-delivery theory predicts that the design principles will not have a positive effect, so the same level of noneffects should occur for both low- and high-spatial learners and for both low- and high-knowledge learners. These predictions are not supported in the research reported in this chapter.

It is interesting to note that knowledge and spatial ability seem to act in opposite ways. Knowledge compensates for poor instructional design, so high-knowledge learners can build understanding with either well-designed or poorly designed instruction, but low-knowledge learners perform much better with well-designed than with poorly designed instruction. In contrast, spatial ability enhances good instruction, so low- and high-spatial learners both perform poorly when instruction is poorly designed but high-spatial learners show a bigger improvement than do low-spatial learners when well-designed instruction is presented.

What is the relation between the individual-differences principle and the multimedia principle (as described in chapter 4), the spatial-contiguity principle (as described in chapter 5), or the temporal-contiguity principle (as described in chapter 6)? The results reported in this chapter suggest that at least in some cases, the multimedia, spatial-contiguity, and temporal-contiguity principles depend on the individual difference characteristics of the learner. In other words, the multimedia, spatial-contiguity, and temporal-contiguity effects may be stronger for certain kinds of learners than for others. Because our results are preliminary, much more research is needed to fully understand the role of individual differences in multimedia learning.

Are there other important individual differences factors? In general, research findings on individual differences has been disappointing partly because it is hard to define individual differences dimensions and partly because it is hard to measure them. Some worthwhile venues for future research include the role of visual and verbal working memory capacity and the role of visual and verbal learning-style preferences.

Implications for Multimedia Design

Research on individual differences in multimedia design effectiveness allows us to tentatively propose a design principle: When working with low-experience and high-spatial learners, be particularly careful to employ relevant principles of multimedia design. This principle should not be taken to mean that good design is irrelevant for high-knowledge or low-spatial learners but rather that it is particularly important for low-knowledge and high-spatial learners.

What are the practical implications of the individual differences effect for knowledge? There are three possible instructional implications: individualization, multiple methods, and pretraining. In the individualization approach, you could design one kind of presentation for low-knowledge learners (based on the principles described in this book) and a different kind of presentation for high-knowledge learners (based on somewhat different principles). What's wrong with this seemingly reasonable approach? The approach may be somewhat difficult to implement because a mistake in classifying a learner can result in providing instruction that is not optimal. In addition, if one kind of presentation results in better learning than does another, then individualization always provides a less desirable kind of learning opportunity for some learners.

In the multiple-methods approach, you could design several different kinds of instruction all in one presentation. In this way, each learner could focus on the kind of method that is most helpful. Unfortunately, we have seen in the chapters on redundancy and coherence effects that adding too much extraneous material can disrupt learning. In this way, the attempt to provide multiple methods could end up creating redundancy and disrupting coherence.

In the pretraining approach, you can determine the skills that are needed to benefit from the instructional message and then give learners practice in those skills. If more knowledge is needed, then pretraining in domain knowledge is called for. If stronger spatial skills are needed, then pretraining in specifically relevant spatial skills is warranted. Once the learner has the appropriate level of pretraining, then the best-quality instructional presentation can be used.

The appropriateness of each approach depends on the specific situation, but in general I prefer the pretraining approach. In this way, all students are exposed to the best-quality instruction and can benefit from it.

This chapter began with the question "For whom does multimedia work?" The preliminary answer is that it seems to work best for low-knowledge and high-spatial learners. However, much additional research is needed to fully understand the role of individual differences in multimedia learning. In particular, research is needed to pinpoint the role of various aspects of spatial ability and verbal ability.

SUGGESTED READINGS

*Mayer, R. E., & Gallini, J. (1990). When is an illustration worth ten thousand words? *Journal of Educational Psychology, 82,* 715–726.

*Mayer, R. E., & Sims, V. K. (1994). For whom is a picture worth a thousand words? Extensions of a dual-coding theory of multimedia learning. *Journal of Educational Psychology, 86,* 389–401.

*Mayer, R. E., Steinhoff, K., Bower, G., & Mars, R. (1995). A generative theory of textbook design: Using annotated illustrations to foster meaningful learning of science text. *Educational Technology Research and Development, 43,* 31–43.

---

* Asterisk indicates that part of the chapter is based on this publication.

11

Principles of Multimedia Design

This chapter summarizes seven principles of multimedia design: multimedia, spatial contiguity, temporal contiguity, coherence, modality, redundancy, and individual differences. It addresses five questions about multimedia design: Does multimedia work? When does multimedia work? For whom does multimedia work? How does multimedia work? What makes an effective multimedia presentation? Finally, the chapter closes with comments concerning the contributions and challenges of multimedia research.

■■ Chapter Outline

SEVEN PRINCIPLES OF MULTIMEDIA DESIGN
FIVE QUESTIONS ABOUT MULTIMEDIA
   Does Multimedia Work?
   When Does Multimedia Work?
   For Whom Does Multimedia Work?
   How Does Multimedia Work?
   What Makes an Effective Multimedia Presentation?
THE CONTRIBUTIONS AND CHALLENGES OF RESEARCH ON
MULTIMEDIA LEARNING

SEVEN PRINCIPLES OF MULTIMEDIA DESIGN

My goal in writing this book was twofold: to improve our understanding of how people learn from words and pictures (that is, to contribute to a theory of multimedia learning) and to improve the design of multimedia presentations (that is, to contribute to the practice of multimedia instruction). On the theoretical side, I began with a cognitive theory of multimedia learning – as described in chapter 3 – that made specific predictions concerning seven kinds design effects. I tested the predicted design effects in a large series of experimental studies, involving measures of both transfer and retention. Overall, the results are highly consistent with the predictions of the cognitive theory of multimedia learning, lending support to our conception of how people integrate visual and verbal presentations (Mayer, 1997, 1999a, 1999b).

On the practical side, the results offer a set of seven basic principles for the design of multimedia presentations. Figure 11.1 defines each of the seven principles of multimedia design that I have presented in this book. The principles are presented as prescriptions for how to design multimedia presentations, but I do not intend the principles to stand alone as a to-be-memorized list of procedures. Rather, I intend for each principle to be implemented in light of the cognitive theory of multimedia learning that I presented in chapter 3; that is, the principles should be used in ways that are consistent with what we know about how people learn from words and pictures.

For each of the seven design principles in Figure 11.1, there are two pieces of empirical evidence – a retention effect in which I compare the retention-test performance of two treatment groups and a transfer effect in which I compare the transfer-test performance of two treatment groups. The two treatment groups consist of one that learns from

---

1. *Multimedia Principle:* Students learn better from words and pictures than from words alone.
2. *Spatial Contiguity Principle:* Students learn better when corresponding words and pictures are presented near rather than far from each other on the page or screen.
3. *Temporal Contiguity Principle:* Students learn better when corresponding words and pictures are presented simultaneously rather than successively.
4. *Coherence Principle:* Students learn better when extraneous words, pictures, and sounds are excluded rather than included.
5. *Modality Principle:* Students learn better from animation and narration than from animation and on-screen text.
6. *Redundancy Principle:* Students learn better from animation and narration than from animation, narration, and on-screen text.
7. *Individual Differences Principle:* Design effects are stronger for low-knowledge learners than for high-knowledge learners and for high-spatial learners rather than for low-spatial learners.

Figure 11.1   Seven research-based principles for the design of multimedia messages.

a multimedia presentation that is based on the design principle and one that learns from a multimedia presentation that is not based on the design principle. On the retention test, the learner is asked to write down an explanation based on the presentation. On the problem-solving transfer test, the learner is asked to write possible solutions to new problems. In short, I examine the effect on retention and on transfer of implementing the design principle.

Figure 11.2 summarizes the empirical evidence based on retention tests that my colleagues and I have administered concerning each of the seven principles. The left column presents the name of the effect and describes the effect in words; the second column lists the median

Design Principle	ES	Gain	Tests
1. *Multimedia effect for retention:* Better retention when learners receive words and corresponding pictures rather than words alone.	.67	23	6 of 9
2. *Spatial contiguity effect for retention:* Better retention when corresponding words and pictures are near rather than far from each other.	.95	42	2 of 2
3. *Temporal contiguity effect for retention:* No better retention when corresponding animation-and-narration segments are simultaneous (or alternating short segments) rather than successive.	.03	00	6 of 8
4. *Coherence effect for retention:* Better retention when extraneous words, sounds, and pictures are excluded rather than included.	1.98	126	11 of 11
5. *Modality effect for retention:* Better retention when words are presented as narration rather than as on-screen text.	.84	30	4 of 4
6. *Redundancy effect for retention:* Better retention when words are presented as narration rather than as narration and on-screen text.	.77	28	2 of 2
7. *Individual differences effect for retention:* Stronger design effects for low- rather than for high-knowledge learners.	.60	157	2 of 3

Figure 11.2 Median effect size (ES) and median percent gain (Gain) on retention test score due to implementing design principles for multimedia messages.

effect size; the third column lists the median percentage gain; and the fourth column lists how many tests confirmed the effect and how many tests were conducted.

Figure 11.3 summarizes the corresponding empirical tests for the seven effects on transfer.

FIVE QUESTIONS ABOUT MULTIMEDIA

The material summarized in Figures 11.1, 11.2, and 11.3 provide some answers to these five questions about multimedia: Does multimedia work? When does multimedia work? For whom does multimedia work? How does multimedia work? What makes an effective multimedia presentation?

Design Principle	ES	Gain	Tests
1. *Multimedia effect for transfer:* Better transfer when learners receive words and corresponding pictures rather than words alone.	1.50	89	9 of 9
2. *Spatial contiguity effect for transfer:* Better transfer when corresponding words and pictures are near rather than far from each other.	1.12	68	5 of 5
3. *Temporal Contiguity effect for transfer:* Better transfer when corresponding animation and narration segments are simultaneous (or alternating short segments) rather than successive.	1.30	60	8 of 8
4. *Coherence effect for transfer:* Better transfer when extraneous words, sounds, and pictures are excluded rather than included.	1.17	82	10 of 11
5. *Modality effect for transfer:* Better transfer when words are presented as narration rather than as on-screen text.	1.17	80	4 of 4
6. *Redundancy effect for transfer:* Better transfer when words are presented as narration rather than as narration and on-screen text.	1.24	79	2 of 2
7. *Individual differences effect for transfer:* Stronger design effects for low- rather than for high-knowledge learners.	.80	61	4 of 4
Stronger design effects for high- rather than for low-knowledge learners.	1.13	46	2 of 2

Figure 11.3 Median effect size (ES) and median percent gain (Gain) on transfer test score due to implementing design principles for multimedia messages

Does Multimedia Work?

A preliminary question concerns whether multimedia works. To answer this question, we must begin by defining what is meant by *multimedia* and what is meant by saying that it works. Our definition of *multimedia* is simple: Multimedia presentations consist of coordinated verbal and visual messages. In contrast, we can compare a multimedia presentation to one that consists of solely a verbal message. In short, we can restate the question this way: "Is it better to learn from words and pictures than from words alone?"

Our definition of whether a multimedia presentation "works" is based on two dependent measures – transfer and retention. We measure whether multimedia works by determining whether it promotes transfer – being able to use the material in the presentation to solve new problems – and whether it promotes retention – being able to remember the important verbal material in the presentation. In short, we restate the question this way: "Do students who learn from words and pictures perform better on transfer and retention tests than students who learn from words alone?"

The multimedia principle, the first principle listed in Figure 11.1, addresses this question. As can be seen in the first lines of Figures 11.2 and 11.3, students perform better on tests of transfer and retention when they learn from words and pictures than from words alone. These results provide clear and consistent evidence that multimedia works; that is, it is better to present a multimedia explanation using both words and pictures than using words alone.

When Does Multimedia Work?

The question of whether multimedia works is a bit too superficial, because not all multimedia messages are equally effective. A deeper question concerns the conditions under which multimedia presentations work; that is, "When does multimedia work?" The bulk of the research presented in this book addresses this crucial question.

Overall, our research allows us to identify five conditions that lead to effective multimedia presentations: (1) spatial contiguity – when corresponding words and pictures are presented near rather than far from each other on the page or screen; (2) temporal contiguity – when corresponding words and pictures are presented simultaneously rather than successively in time; (3) coherence – when extraneous words, sounds, and pictures are minimized; (4) modality – when words are presented as speech rather than as text in multimedia presentations; and (5) redundancy – when words are presented as speech rather than as speech and text in multimedia presentations. These principles are summarized in the second through sixth principles of Figure 11.1. The research summarized in the second through sixth lines of Figures 11.2 and 11.3 provides consistent evidence that multimedia messages result in better transfer and retention under these five conditions.

Another condition that is beginning to receive some preliminary research support in our labatory is the personalization effect: Multimedia messages result in better transfer performance (but not retention) when the verbal material is presented in a conversational style – using first and second person – than when the identical verbal material is presented in a nonconversational style – using third person. In two studies on the lightning presentation conducted by Roxana Moreno and me, students who received personalized voice or text performed better on transfer than did students who received nonpersonalized voice or text (Moreno & Mayer, in press). One interpretation consistent with the cognitive theory of multimedia learning and with other research on personalization (Reeves & Nass, 1996) is that students work harder to make sense of the material when they feel they are engaged in a social interaction.

Finally, we are also beginning to find some preliminary research support for an interactivity effect: Multimedia messages result in better transfer performance (but not retention) when learners are able to control the pace of presentation. In a study conducted by Paul Chandler and me, we created an interactivity treatment in which the lightning presentation was broken down into sixteen short segments, each containing a sentence or two as well as ten to fifteen seconds of corresponding animation. Students could go on to the next segment by clicking on a button labeled "Click here to continue." Results from our first study show that students who were able to control the presentation pace – by clicking on a button to receive each of sixteen segments – performed better on transfer tests than did students who received the entire presentation as a continuous unit. One interpretation consistent with the cognitive theory of multimedia learning and with other research on interactivity (Rieber, 1994) is that students can avoid overloading their working memory when they control the presentation rate.

Although these results concerning personalization and interactivity effects are too preliminary to be included as principles in Figure 11.1, they may eventually form the basis for further answers to the question of *when* multimedia works.

For Whom Does Multimedia Work?

Much less is known concerning the question of who learns best from multimedia. The final principle listed in Figure 11.1 states that well-designed multimedia presentations work best for learners who are low rather than high in prior knowledge about the subject matter and for learners who are high rather than low in spatial ability. The final lines in Figures 11.2 and 11.3 summarize empirical evidence that well-designed multimedia presentations result in higher transfer and retention performance for certain kinds of learners than for others. Although these results are preliminary, they show how the design principles need to be qualified with respect to different kinds of learners. Additional research is needed to pinpoint the role of individual differences in multimedia learning.

How Does Multimedia Work?

Our results are most consistent with a cognitive theory of multimedia learning, which is based on three assumptions – that people have separate visual and auditory channels; that the channels are limited in capacity; and that meaningful learning involves actively selecting, organizing, and integrating incoming visual and auditory information. Each of the design effects summarized in Figures 11.1, 11.2, and 11.3 is consistent with the cognitive theory of multimedia learning.

First, the cognitive theory of multimedia learning helps to explain the multimedia effect. When only words are presented, then the most likely cognitive processes are selecting words, organizing words, and integrating words with prior knowledge. When both words and pictures are presented, then learners can also engage in selecting images, organizing images, and integrating words and images. The process of integrating relevant words and images is a key step in meaningful learning and is facilitated by presenting an explanation using words and pictures rather than using words alone.

Second, the cognitive theory of multimedia learning helps to explain the spatial contiguity effect. When corresponding words and pictures are separated from one another on the page, the learner is less likely to be able to hold corresponding verbal and visual representations in working memory at the same time. In contrast, when corresponding words and pictures are presented next to one another on the page, the learner is more likely to be able to hold corresponding verbal and visual representations in working memory at the same time. Thus, the process of integrating relevant words and images is more likely to occur when words and pictures are integrated rather than separated.

Third, the cognitive theory of multimedia learning helps to explain the temporal contiguity effect. When corresponding words and pictures are separated from one another in time, the learner is less likely to be able to hold corresponding verbal and visual representations in working memory at the same time. In contrast, when corresponding words and pictures are presented simultaneously, the learner is more likely to be able to hold corresponding verbal and visual representations in working memory at the same time. Again, the process of integrating relevant words and images is facilitated for simultaneous rather than successive presentation.

Fourth, the cognitive theory of multimedia learning helps to explain the coherence effect. When extraneous material is presented, working memory may become cluttered with irrelevant words and/or irrelevant images, making it more difficult to hold corresponding relevant words and images in working memory at the same time. In contrast, when only relevant material is presented, working memory is more likely to hold corresponding relevant words and images at the same time. This situation facilitates a key step in meaningful learning – namely, integrating corresponding words and images.

Fifth, the cognitive theory of multimedia learning can account for the modality and redundancy effects. When words are presented as text, they must compete for visual attention with the animation in the visual channel, creating what can be called *split attention*. In short, visual attention is split between the animation and the text, resulting in less relevant material being selected for further processing. In contrast, when words are presented as speech, they can be processed in the auditory channel, thus freeing the visual channel for processing of the animation. This situation is most likely to promote key steps in meaningful learning, including integrating corresponding words and pictures.

Finally, the individual differences effects we obtained are also consistent with the cognitive theory of multimedia learning. High-knowledge learners may be able to create and use images on their own, so they do not need well-designed multimedia presentations. In contrast, low-knowledge learners may need to have images supplied to them and therefore are more likely to benefit from multimedia presentations. Multimedia learning may require good spatial cognition skills, so good multimedia design is more likely to help high- rather than low-spatial learners. Low-spatial learners may require so much mental energy to hold images in their working memory that they do not have capacity left over to mentally integrate the words and pictures. In contrast, high-spatial learners may have sufficient mental energy to hold images and also be able to coordinate them with verbal representations.

In no case did we find support for the information-delivery theory, in which visual and verbal modes of presentation are viewed as two delivery channels. The information-delivery metaphor does not seem to be a productive one for the design of effective multimedia messages.

Instead, I view multimedia learners as active sense makers who actively process the incoming words and pictures through visual and auditory channels that are highly limited in capacity. To understand multimedia design, it seems essential to begin with a coherent theory of how people learn from words and pictures.

What Makes an Effective Multimedia Presentation?

Our work allows us to suggest the characteristics of an effective multimedia presentation. To begin, let's focus only on computer-based multimedia presentations that seek to explain how something works using animation with narration. First, the presentation should consist of both words and pictures – that is, narration and animation rather than narration alone. In short, the presentation should be multimedia. Second, corresponding portions of the animation and narration should be presented simultaneously in time. In short, the presentation should be integrated. Third, only the core cause-and-effect explanation should be presented, without extraneous words, sounds, or pictures. In short, the presentation should be concise. Fourth, the words should be presented as speech (i.e., narration) rather than as text (i.e., on-screen text) or as speech and text. In short, the presentation should be channeled, – with words directed toward the auditory channel and pictures directed toward the visual channel. Finally, the material itself should have a potentially meaningful structure – such as a cause-and-effect chain. Thus, the most effective computer-based multimedia presentation is a *concise narrated animation* (CNA), which I define as a concise narration describing the cause-and-effect system coordinated with a concise animation depicting the cause-and-effect system. In short, CNAs are the building blocks of effective computer-based multimedia messages. The characteristics of CNAs are summarized in Figure 11.4. This analysis helps to extend Rieber's (1990a, 1990b) earlier work on the potential of animation as an aid to computer-based instruction.

Similarly, let's examine the characteristics of effective book-based multimedia presentations, consisting of text and illustrations. First, the presentation should consist of both words and pictures – that is, text and illustrations rather than text alone. In short, the presentation should be multimedia. Second, corresponding portions of the text and illustration should be presented next to each other on the page. In short, the presentation should be integrated. Third, the core cause-and-effect explanation should be presented, without extraneous text and illustrations. The illustration must consist of a series of frames depicting various states of the system, and each frame should include text describing the state of the system in words. Finally, the material itself

Figure 11.4   Features of a Concise Narrated Animation

Features	Description
Multimedia	Includes corresponding animation and narration rather than narration alone
Integrated	Corresponding animation and narration are presented simultaneously rather than successively
Concise	Extraneous words, pictures, and sounds are excluded rather than included
Channeled	Words are presented as speech rather than on-screen text (or both speech and on-screen text)
Structured	Includes series of narrated animation segments describing key steps in the process (for cause-and-effect material)

should have a potentially meaningful structure – such as a cause-and-effect chain. Thus, the most effective book-based multimedia presentation is a concise annotated illustration (CAI), which I define as a concise series of frames, each with concise coordinated text captions. In short, CAIs are the building blocks of effective book-based multimedia presentations. Figure 11.5 summarizes the characteristics of CAIs. This analysis helps to extend earlier research on the potential of illustrations in text-based instruction (Mandl & Levin, 1989; Schnotz & Kulhavy, 1994; Willows & Houghton, 1987).

THE CONTRIBUTIONS AND CHALLENGES OF RESEARCH ON MULTIMEDIA LEARNING

Suppose you want to create a multimedia presentation to be delivered via the World Wide Web. What would be your criteria for building the presentation? Certainly, an important criterion is content – you want to

Figure 11.5   Features of Concise Annotated Illustrations

Features	Description
Multimedia	Includes corresponding text and illustrations rather than text alone
Integrated	Corresponding text and illustrations are presented near rather than far from each other
Concise	Extraneous words and pictures are excluded rather than included
Structured	Includes series of annotated illustration frames describing key steps in the process (for cause-and-effect material)

make sure it presents the information that you intend to convey. Another criterion is aesthetics – you want to make sure the presentation looks good. Finally, another criterion is sophistication – you want to make sure the presentation takes advantage of the latest technological developments.

Yet if you designed a technologically sophisticated, aesthetically pleasing, information-rich presentation, you would have failed to take into account an important human criterion: Is the presentation designed to be compatible with the way that people learn from words and pictures? This book is concerned with this human criterion and with the premise that multimedia design can be based on scientific research and theory. In short, an important criterion for multimedia design concerns what people learn from the presentation.

Can multimedia design be based on scientific research? In many cases, recommendations for multimedia design are based on intuitions rather than scientific research. Clearly, the intuitions of thoughtful scholars have a place. Perhaps the best known and most acclaimed work in this area is Edward Tufte's work on the design of data graphics, which he calls "principles of information design" (Tufte, 1990, p. 10). For example, Tufte (1983, 1990) provides many useful suggestions for how to design data graphics such as charts, tables, diagrams, and graphs. For example, like the contiguity principle proposed in this book, Tufte (1990) states that "words and pictures belong together." Yet he offers no empirical or theoretical justification. Similarly, Horn (1998, p. 8) calls for the development of a visual language based on "the integration of words, images, and shapes into a single communication unit."

The goal of this book is to offer a scientific approach to the development of design principles. The advantage of this approach is that it allows us to determine whether the principles work, but a disadvantage is that it causes us to narrow our focus. In this book, I summarize a systematic program of research aimed at understanding how people learn from words and pictures that explain how something works. The work is limited to short, causal explanations, to learning by college students, and to a few fundamental principles. Yet even this modest examination required approximately 10 years of concentrated study by a multidisciplinary team of cognitive psychologists, educational technology experts, and computer scientists. This project demonstrates that it is possible to formulate testable questions about multimedia learning, it is possible to conduct scientifically rigorous research to answer the questions, and it is possible to develop a cognitive theory of multimedia learning to guide the research. In short, an important outcome of this project is a demonstration of how it is possible to create design principles based on empirical research and cognitive theory.

What needs to be done? Research in multimedia learning is in its infancy. The major challenges are to create a useful base of empirical research and cognitive theory. The ultimate goal should be to systematize design principles based on empirical research and a comprehensive theory. Although multimedia explanations are an important type of multimedia message, there are many other uses of multimedia that require study. The field of study needs to include a range of multimedia learning situations, a range of learners, and a range of design principles. Because the goal of multimedia learning is usually meaningful learning, it is worthwhile to use measures of learning that are sensitive to learner understanding, like the transfer measures used throughout this book. In addition, because working memory load plays a central part in the cognitive theory of multimedia learning, it would be useful to have more direct measures of cognitive load during learning, including paper-and-pencil surveys (Paas & Van Merrienboer, 1994). It would also be helpful to conduct research aimed at understanding the role of individual differences. Increasing interest on personalizing instructional episodes – such as through the use of on-screen pedagogic agents – suggests the need for additional research on the role of personalization in multimedia design. Often, multimedia presentations allow for user interaction and exploration, so additional research is needed on the role of interactivity in multimedia learning.

In summary, multimedia learning offers a potentially powerful way for people to understand things that would be very difficult to grasp from words alone. This book demonstrates the potential benefits of learning that involves the structured integration of words and pictures. It offers a glimpse of how we can improve on verbal messages, which have become the basis for most instruction. It offers a vision of the potential of multimedia instructional messages to improve human understanding. I will consider this book a success if it helps to promote a better understanding of how to foster meaningful learning through the integration of words and pictures.

SUGGESTED READINGS

Mayer, R. E. (1999a). Multimedia aids to problem-solving transfer. *International Journal of Educational Research, 31*, 611–623.

Mayer, R. E. (1999b). Research-based principles for the design of instructional messages: The case of multimedia explanations. *Document Design, 1*, 7–20.

References

Alwitt, L. F., Anderson, D. R., Lorch, E. P., & Levin, S. R. (1980). Preschool children's visual attention to attributes of television. *Human Communication Research, 7,* 52–67.

Anderson, D. R., & Lorch, E. P. (1983). Looking at television: Action or reaction? In J. Bryant & D. R. Anderson (Eds.), *Children's understanding of television: Research on attention and comprehension* (pp. 1–33). New York: Academic Press.

Baddeley, A. D. (1986). *Working memory.* Oxford, England: Oxford University Press.

Baddeley, A. D. (1992). Working memory. *Science, 255,* 556–559.

Baddeley, A. D. (1999). *Human memory.* Boston: Allyn & Bacon.

Baggett, P. (1984). Role of temporal overlap of visual and auditory material in forming dual media associations. *Journal of Educational Psychology, 76,* 408–417.

Baggett, P. (1989). Understanding visual and verbal messages. In H. Mandl & J. R. Levin (Eds.), *Knowledge acquisition from text and pictures* (pp. 101–124). Amsterdam: Elsevier.

Baggett, P., & Ehrenfeucht, A. (1983). Encoding and retaining information in the visuals and verbals of an educational movie. *Educational Communications and Technology Journal, 31,* 23–32.

Bobis, J., Sweller, J., & Cooper, M. (1993). Cognitive load effects in a primary school geometry task. *Learning and Instruction, 3,* 1–21.

Bransford, J. D., Brown, A. L., & Cocking, R. R. (1999). *How people learn.* Washington, DC: National Academy Press.

Britton, B. K., Woodward, A., & Binkley, M. (Eds.). (1993). *Learning from textbooks: Theory and practice.* Hillsdale, NJ: Erlbaum.

Calvert, S. L., & Scott, M. C. (1989). Sound effects for children's temporal integration of fast-paced television content. *Journal of Broadcasting and Electronic Media, 33,* 233–246.

Carroll, J. B. (1993). *Human cognitive abilities*. Cambridge, England: Cambridge University Press.

Chambliss, M. J., & Calfee, R. C. (1998). *Textbooks for learning*. Oxford, England: Blackwell.

Chandler, P., & Sweller, J. (1991). Cognitive load theory and the format of instruction. *Cognition and Instruction, 8,* 293–332.

Chandler, P., & Sweller, J. (1992). The split-attention effect as a factor in the design of instruction. *British Journal of Educational Psychology, 62,* 233–246.

Chi, M. T. H., Bassok, M., Lewis, M. W., Reimann, P., & Glaser, R. (1989). Self-explanations: How students study and use examples in learning to solve problems. *Cognitive Science, 13,* 145–182.

Clark, J. M., & Paivio, A. (1991). Dual coding theory and education. *Educational Psychology Review, 3,* 149–210.

Clark, R. E. (1983). Reconsidering research on learning from media. *Review of Educational Research, 53*(2), 445–459.

Clark, R. E. (1994). Media will never influence learning. *Educational Technology Research and Development, 42,* 21–30.

Clark, R. E., & Salomon, G. (1986). Media in teaching. In M. C. Wittrock (Ed.), *Handbook of research on teaching* (3rd ed., pp. 464–478). New York: Macmillan.

Cognition and Technology Group at Vanderbilt (1996). Looking at technology in context: A framework for understanding technology and education. In D. C. Berliner & R. C. Calfee (Eds.), *Handbook of educational psychology* (pp. 807–840). New York: Macmillan.

Cook, L. K., & Mayer, R. E. (1988). Teaching readers about the structure of scientific text. *Journal of Educational Psychology, 80,* 448–456.

Cooper, G., & Sweller, J. (1987). The effects of schema acquisition and rule automation on mathematical problem-solving transfer. *Journal of Educational Psychology, 79,* 347–362.

Cronbach, L. J., & Snow, R. E. (1977). *Aptitudes and instructional methods.* New York: Irvington.

Cuban, L. (1986). *Teachers and machines: The classroom use of technology since 1920.* New York: Teachers College Press.

Dewey, J. (1913). *Interest and effort in education.* Cambridge, MA: Houghton Mifflin.

Ekstrom, R. B., French, J. W., & Harman, H. H. (1976). *Manual for kit of factor-referenced cognitive tests.* Princeton, NJ: Educational Testing Service.

Fleming, M., & Levie, W. H. (Eds.). (1993). *Instructional message design: Principles from the behavioral and cognitive sciences* (2nd ed). Englewood Cliffs, NJ: Educational Technology Publications.

Garner, R., Alexander, P., Gillingham, M., Kulikowich, J., & Brown, R. (1991). Interest and learning from text. *American Educational Research Journal, 28,* 643–659.

Garner, R., Brown, R., Sanders, S., & Menke, D. (1992). Seductive details and learning from text. In K. A. Renninger, S. Hidi, & A. Krapp (Eds.), *The role of interest in learning and development* (pp. 239–254). Hillsdale, NJ: Erlbaum.

Garner, R., Gillingham, M., & White, C. (1989). Effects of seductive details on macroprocessing and microprocessing in adults and children. *Cognition and Instruction, 6,* 41–57.

Harp, S. F., & Mayer, R. E. (1997). The role of interest in learning from scientific text and illustrations: On the distinction between emotional interest and cognitive interest. *Journal of Educational Psychology, 89,* 92–102.

Harp, S. F., & Mayer, R. E. (1998). How seductive details do their damage: A theory of cognitive interest in science learning. *Journal of Educational Psychology, 90,* 414–434.

Hegarty, M., Carpenter, P., A., & Just, M. A. (1996). Diagrams in the comprehension of scientific texts. In R. Barr, M. L. Kamil, P. Mosenthal, & P. D. Pearson (Eds.), *Handbook of reading research. Volume II* (pp. 641–668). Mahwah, NJ: Erlbaum.

Hidi, S., & Anderson, V. (1992). Situational interest and its impact on reading expository writing. In K. A. Renninger, S. Hidi, & A. Krapp (Eds.), *The role of interest in learning and development* (pp. 215–238). Hillsdale, NJ: Erlbaum.

Hidi, S., & Baird, W. (1986). Interestingness: A neglected variable in discourse processing. *Cognitive Science, 10,* 179–94.

Hidi, S., & Baird, W. (1988). Strategies for increasing text-based interest and students' recall of expository text. *Reading Research Quarterly, 23,* 465–483.

Horn, R. E. (1998). *Visual language.* Bainbridge Island, WA: MacroVU.

Jonassen, D. H., Campbell, J. P., & Davidson, M. E. (1994). Learning with media: Restructuring the debate. *Educational Technology Research and Development, 42* (2), 20–38.

Jonassen, D. H., & Grabowski, B. L. (1993). *Handbook of individual differences, learning, and instruction.* Hillsdale, NJ: Erlbaum.

Jonassen, D. H., & Reeves, T. C. (1996). Learning with technology: Using computers as cognitive tools. In D. H. Jonassen (Ed.), *Handbook of research for educational communication and technology* (pp. 693–719). New York: Macmillan.

Kalyuga, S., Chandler, P., & Sweller, J. (1998). Levels of expertise and instructional design. *Human Factors, 40,* 1–17.

Kalyuga, S., Chandler, P., & Sweller, P. (1999). Managing split-attention and redundancy in multimedia instruction. *Applied Cognitive Psychology, 13,* 351–372.

Kalyuga, S., Chandler, P., & Sweller, J. (2000). Incorporating learner experience into the design of multimedia instruction. *Journal of Educational Psychology, 92,* 126–136.

Kintsch, W. (1980). Learning from text, levels of comprehension, or: Why would anyone read a story anyway? *Poetics, 9,* 87–98.

Kozma, R. B. (1991). Learning with media. *Review of Educational Research, 61,* 179–211.

Kozma, R. B. (1994). Will media influence learning? Reframing the debate. *Educational Technology Research and Development, 42* (2), 7–19.

Lambert, N. M., & McCombs, B. L. (1998). *How students learn*. Washington, DC: American Psychological Association.

Landauer, T. K. (1995). *The trouble with computers*. Cambridge, MA: MIT Press.

Leutner, D., & Plass, J. L. (1998). Measuring learning styles with questionnaires versus direct observation of preferential choice behavior in authentic learning situations: The Visualizer/Verbalizer Behavior Observation Scale (VV-BOS). *Computers in Human Behavior, 14*, 543–557.

Levin, J. R., & Mayer, R. E. (1993). Understanding illustrations in text. In B. K. Britton, A. Woodward, & M. Binkley (Eds.), *Learning from textbooks: Theory and practice* (pp. 95–113). Hillsdale, NJ: Erlbaum.

Mandl, H., & Levin, J. R. (Eds.) (1989). *Knowledge acquisition from text and pictures*. Amsterdam: North-Holland.

Mayer, R. E. (1983). Can you repeat that? Qualitative effects of repetition and advance organizers on learning from science prose. *Journal of Educational Psychology, 75*, 40–49.

Mayer, R. E. (1989a). Models for understanding. *Review of Educational Research, 59*, 43–64.

Mayer, R. E. (1989b). Systematic thinking fostered by illustrations in scientific text. *Journal of Educational Psychology, 81*, 240–246.

Mayer, R. E. (1993a). Problem-solving principles. In M. Fleming & W. H. Levie (Eds.), *Instructional message design: Principles from behavioral and cognitive sciences* (2nd ed., pp. 253–282). Englewood Cliffs, NJ: Educational Technology Publications.

Mayer, R. E. (1993b). Illustrations that instruct. In R. Glaser (Ed.), *Advances in instructional psychology* (vol. 4, pp. 253–284). Hillsdale, NJ: Erlbaum.

Mayer, R. E. (1996). Learning strategies for making sense out of expository text: The SOI model for guiding three cognitive processes in knowledge construction. *Educational Psychology Review, 8*, 357–371.

Mayer, R. E. (1997). Multimedia learning: Are we asking the right questions? *Educational Psychologist, 32*, 1–19.

Mayer, R. E. (1999a). Multimedia aids to problem-solving transfer. *International Journal of Educational Research, 31*, 611–623.

Mayer, R. E. (1999b). Research-based principles for the design of instructional messages: The case of multimedia explanations. *Document Design, 1*, 7–20.

Mayer, R. E. (1999c). *The promise of educational psychology*. Upper Saddle River, NJ: Prentice Hall/Merrill.

Mayer, R. E., & Anderson, R. B. (1991). Animations need narrations: An experimental test of a dual-coding hypothesis. *Journal of Educational Psychology, 83*, 484–490.

Mayer, R. E., & Anderson, R. B. (1992). The instructive animation: Helping students build connections between words and pictures in multimedia learning. *Journal of Educational Psychology, 84*, 444–452.

Mayer, R. E., Bove, W., Bryman, A., Mars, R., & Tapangco, L. (1996). When less is more: Meaningful learning from visual and verbal summaries of science textbook lessons. *Journal of Educational Psychology, 88,* 64–73.

Mayer, R. E., & Gallini, J. (1990). When is an illustration worth ten thousand words? *Journal of Educational Psychology, 82,* 715–726.

Mayer, R. E., Heiser, J., & Lonn, S. (in press). Cognitive constraints on multimedia learning: When presenting more material results in less understanding. *Journal of Educational Psychology.*

Mayer, R. E., & Moreno, R. (1998). A split-attention effect in multimedia learning: Evidence for dual processing systems in working memory. *Journal of Educational Psychology, 90,* 312–320.

Mayer, R. E., Moreno, R., Boire, M., & Vagge, S. (1999). Maximizing constructivist learning from multimedia communications by minimizing cognitive load. *Journal of Educational Psychology, 91,* 638–643.

Mayer, R. E., & Sims, V. K. (1994). For whom is a picture worth a thousand words? Extensions of a dual-coding theory of multimedia learning. *Journal of Educational Psychology, 84,* 389–401.

Mayer, R. E., Sims, V., & Tajika, H. (1995). A comparison of how textbooks teach mathematical problem solving in Japan and the United States. *American Educational Research Journal, 32,* 443–460.

Mayer, R. E., Steinhoff, K., Bower, G., & Mars, R. (1995). A generative theory of textbook design: Using annotated illustrations to foster meaningful learning of science text. *Educational Technology Research and Development, 43*(1), 31–43.

Miller, G. A. (1956). The magic number seven, plus or minus two: Some limits on our capacity for processing information. *Psychological Review, 63,* 81–97.

Mohr, P., Glover, J., & Ronning, R. R. (1984). The effect of related and unrelated details on the recall of major ideas in prose. *Journal of Reading Behavior, 16,* 97–109.

Moreno, R., & Mayer, R. E. (1999). Cognitive principles of multimedia learning: The role of modality and contiguity. *Journal of Educational Psychology, 91,* 358–368.

Moreno, R., & Mayer, R. E. (2000). A coherence effect in multimedia learning: The case for minimizing irrelevant sounds in the design of multimedia messages. *Journal of Educational Psychology, 92,* 117–125.

Moreno, R., & Mayer, R. E. (in press). Engaging students in active learning: The case for personalized multimedia messages. *Journal of Educational Psychology.*

Mousavi, S., Low, R., & Sweller, J. (1995). Reducing cognitive load by mixing auditory and visual presentation modes. *Journal of Educational Psychology, 87,* 319–334.

Norman, D. A. (1993). *Things that make us smart.* Reading, MA: Addison-Wesley.

Paas, F. G. W. C., & Van Merrienboer, J. J. G. (1994). Measurement of cognitive load in instructional research. *Perceptual & Motor Skills, 79,* 419–430.

Paivio, A. (1986). *Mental representations: A dual coding approach.* Oxford, England: Oxford University Press.

Plass, J. L., Chun, D. M., Mayer, R. E., & Leutner, D. (1998). Supporting visual and verbal learning preferences in a second language multimedia learning environment. *Journal of Educational Psychology, 90,* 25–36.

Reder, L. M., Anderson, J. R. (1980). A comparison of texts and their summaries: Memorial consequences. *Journal of Verbal Learning & Verbal Behavior, 19,* 121–134.

Reeves, B., & Nass, C. (1996). *The media equation.* New York: Cambridge University Press.

Rieber, L. P. (1990a). Using computer animated graphics in science instruction with children. *Journal of Educational Psychology, 82,* 135–140.

Rieber, L. P. (1990b). Animation in computer-based instruction. *Educational Technology Research and Development, 38,* 77–86.

Rieber, L. P. (1994). *Computers, graphics, and learning.* Madison, WI: Brown & Benchmark.

Salomon, G. (1994). *Interaction of media, cognition, and learning.* Hillsdale, NJ: Erlbaum.

Schnotz, W., Bannert, M., & Seufert, T. (in press). Supportive and interference effects in multimedia learning. In A. C. Graesser, J. A. Leon, & J. Otero (Eds.), *Psychology of science text comprehension.* Mahwah, NJ: Erlbaum.

Schnotz, W., & Kulhavy, R. W. (1994). *Comprehension of graphics.* Amsterdam: North-Holland.

Shirey, L. (1992). Importance, interest, and selective attention. In K. A. Renninger, S. Hidi, & A. Krapp (Eds.), *The role of interest in learning and development* (pp. 255–277). Hillsdale, NJ: Erlbaum.

Shirey, L., & Reynolds, R. (1988). Effect of interest on attention and learning. *Journal of Educational Psychology, 80,* 159–166.

Simon, H. A. (1974). How big is a chunk? *Science, 183,* 482–488.

Sternberg, R. J. (1990). *Metaphors of mind: Conceptions of the nature of human intelligence.* Cambridge, England: Cambridge University Press.

Sweller, J. (1999). *Instructional design in technical areas.* Camberwell, Australia: ACER Press.

Sweller, J. & Chandler, P. (1994). Why some material is difficult to learn. *Cognition and Instruction, 12,* 185–233.

Sweller, J., Chandler, P., Tierney, P., & Cooper, M. (1990). Cognitive load and selective attention as factors in the structuring of technical material. *Journal of Experimental Psychology: General, 119,* 176–192.

Sweller, J., & Cooper, M. (1985). The use of worked examples as a substitute for problem solving in learning algebra. *Cognition and Instruction, 2,* 59–89.

Tarmizi, R., & Sweller, J. (1988). Guidance during mathematical problem solving. *Journal of Educational Psychology, 80,* 424–436.

Tindall-Ford, S., Chandler, P., & Sweller, J. (1997). When two sensory modes are better than one. *Journal of Experimental Psychology: Applied, 3*, 257–287.

Tufte, E. R. (1983). *Envisioning information.* Cheshire, CT: Graphics Press.

Tufte, E. R. (1990). *The visual display of quantitative information.* Cheshire, CT: Graphics Press.

Wade, S. (1992). How interest affects learning from text. In K. A. Renninger, S. Hidi, & A. Krapp (Eds.), *The role of interest in learning and development* (pp. 255–277). Hillsdale, NJ: Erlbaum.

Wade, S., & Adams, R. (1990). Effects of importance and interest on recall of biographical text. *Journal of Reading Behavior, 22*, 331–353.

Ward, M., & Sweller, J. (1990). Structuring effective worked out examples. *Cognition and Instruction, 7*, 1–39.

Weiner, B. (1990). History of motivational research in education. *Journal of Educational Psychology, 82*, 616–622.

Weiner, B. (1992). Motivation. In M. Alkin (Ed.), *Encyclopedia of educational research* (6th ed; pp. 860–865). New York: Macmillan.

Wetzel, C. D., Radtke, P. H., & Stern, H. W. (1994). *Instructional effectiveness of video media.* Hillsdale, NJ: Erlbaum.

Willows, D. M., & Houghton, H. A. (1987). *The psychology of illustration: Volume 1, Basic research.* New York: Springer-Verlag.

Wittrock, M. C. (1989). Generative processes of comprehension. *Educational Psychologist, 24*, 345–376.

Author Index

Subject Index

active learning, 17–18, 20, 41, 44
active processing, 41, 43–44, 50–53
animation. *See* narrated animation.
annotated illustrations, 24–25, 31–32, 36. *See also* concise annotated illustration.
arousal theory, 117, 124
auditory/verbal channel, 41, 47–48

background music, 124–128
book-based environment, 24–25, 31, 33, 35–36
brakes lesson, 30–35, 40

capacity-limitation hypothesis, 152, 154, 157–158
captioned animation, 136. *See also* on-screen text.
captioned illustrations, 129. *See also* annotated illustrations.
central executive, 50
chunking, 49
cognitive artifacts, 11
cognitive capacity, 49
cognitive interest, 119
cognitive load, 49–50, 194
cognitive processes during learning, 41, 52–58
cognitive resources, 50

cognitive theory of multimedia learning, 41–62, 67–69, 79, 87–88, 93–94, 100–101, 111, 119, 124–125, 129, 137–140, 145, 152–153, 158, 166–167, 171, 177, 179–181, 189–191
coherence, 114
coherence effect, 114, 120–123, 126–132, 185–186
coherence principle, 113–133, 184–186
commodity view of learning, 13
computer-assisted instruction, 9–10
computer-based environment, 24, 26–28, 32–33, 36–37
computer technology, 11
conceptual relevance, 117
concise annotated illustration, 192. *See also* annotated illustration.
concise narrated animation, 135, 146–149, 191–192. *See also* narrated animation.
contiguity effect, 140. *See also* spatial contiguity effect, temporal contiguity effect.

decorative illustrations, 77
delivery media, 1, 5–7
design principles, 8–12, 24, 183–186.
diagrams, 157

207